'Hello. This is the Ambassador of Belgium speaking. How can I help?'

'Hello. I am the fiancée of Charles Bertrand. I am sorry to tell you that Charles passed away in the early hours of this morning.' I was relieved to pass this information on to Charles's friend and country representative.

'Who is Charles?' he said.

'Charles Bertrand.' I thought perhaps he hadn't heard me properly the first time.

'I am sorry. I do not know a Charles Bertrand. I am sorry to hear of your loss. Is there anything I can do?' His voice was concerned and kind.

'Oh, no, I'm sorry to trouble you. You really don't know Charles?' I had to check it.

'No. Is he Belgian?' he enquired.

'Yes, he was. I'm sorry to trouble you. Good-bye.' I replaced the receiver. It was then that my tragedy turned into a nightmare.

Thus begins the harrowing tale at the heart of this important book. Annie Bennett tells her personal story of the consequences of Love Addiction, the events that led up to the revelation that her lover was someone quite different from the person she had so wilfully believed him to be and her painful journey to understanding the addictive cycle she was in.

This story, which will be recognized by so many others who are locked into the same painful cycle of behaviour, forms the basis of Annie Bennett's guide to understanding what Love Addiction is and how to end it.

The Love Trap

The Love Trap

breaking free from Love Addiction

Annie Bennett

Foreword by Kip Flock

Hammersmith Press
London, UK

First published in 2008 by Hammersmith Press Limited
496 Fulham Palace Road, London SW6 6JD, UK
www.hammersmithpress.co.uk

Disclaimer
The central story in this book is the author's own but she has changed all names, including her own, to protect the privacy of the individuals concerned. The story is entirely from the author's subjective perspective and she acknowledges that her interpretation of the behaviour of others may well not match entirely with their own recollection of events. Furthermore, while the advice and information in this book are believed to be true and accurate at the date of going to press, neither the author nor the publisher can accept any legal responsibility or liability for any errors or omissions that may be made. To guide you through difficult periods of personal growth you are strongly advised to seek the help of a qualified therapist.

British Library Cataloguing in Publication Data: A CIP record of this book is available from the British Library.

ISBN 978-1-905140-11-4

Commissioning editor: Georgina Bentliff
Edited by: Anne Charlish
Designed by Julie Bennett
Production by Helen Whitehorn, Pathmedia
Typeset by Phoenix Photosetting, Chatham, Kent, UK
Printed and bound by TJ International Ltd, Padstow, Cornwall, UK
Cover image: Cherubs Tugging Heart © Images.com/Corbis

FSC
Mixed Sources
Product group from well-managed forests and other controlled sources
Cert no. SGS-COC-2482
www.fsc.org
© 1996 Forest Stewardship Council

Contents

ACKNOWLEDGMENTS

The writing of this book started as a way of processing my emotional pain and distress. I have often suggested to my clients that writing about emotional issues is a useful way of processing feelings. Writing can have an extraordinary influence when wanting to let go of emotions. Writing allows us to reconnect to the creative hemisphere of the brain, bypassing logical thought and permitting us to go with the flow of our emotions. For those of us who have learned to close off, or shut down, some of our feelings, writing can be a lifeline; for many it is.

Writing something that will be read by the public has been a major challenge for me as a dyslexic person who believed that I was 'stupid' - a message reinforced by my father. Shame had overcome my internal belief system from an early age and I truly believed that I was intellectually inferior to others. In this regard, I would especially like to acknowledge the gentle and constant support shown me by my publisher Georgina Bentliff and her editor Anne Charlish. At times I have feared they would give up on my literary efforts.

I remember with gratitude the constant reassurances from my colleagues at the Meadows in Arizona, for without their encouragement I surely would not have persevered to tell my story. I thank Peta and Brian Norman for introducing me to Pat and Pia Mellody at the Meadows;

without their kind invitation to spend time with them in Arizona, I would not have had the opportunity of seeing clearly, for the first time, the tangled and dangerous situations in which I had often engaged - all in the name of Love. In particular, I must acknowledge the teaching of Pia Mellody, Patrick Carnes and John Bradshaw, to whose concepts and ideas I have given new expression as the theoretical underpinning to understanding my own personal story.

I would like to acknowledge my dear friend and family support, Bernard - a man who makes no personal judgments and a person who is a great asset to his community. I acknowledge gratitude to my partner Reefe, for being understanding and steadfast; and to Alex Rathbone for spurring me on, giving me confidence that what I was doing was worthwhile. I acknowledge the kind support and guidance of my friend Sarah Conacher. Acknowledgment and thanks also go to my friends and colleagues in Spain, Candi Garcia; Sylvia, Hilton and Jake Knights; Dr Miguel Corty and Michiela; Vince Tracey at Radio OCI; and Jeff at the Round Town News.

I owe enormous gratitude to Kip Flock who continuously challenged me and teased out my hidden shame and encouraged me to expose the secrets from within my family system.

I am eternally grateful to my clients for entrusting me with their deepest feelings; it has been, and remains, a privilege and an honour to work with them.

Annie Bennett
2007

FOREWORD

Rarely has a book been written that shares the vulnerability of the author as well as providing practical help in service to others. *The Love Trap: Breaking Free From Love Addiction* is just such a book. Annie Bennett courageously describes her own struggle with love addiction. She has given us a gift – a glimpse of her own soul emerging out of the agonies of a relationship with a love avoidant partner into the healing of recovery.

As an accomplished psychotherapist, Annie has dedicated herself to leading others out of the distress of being devalued in emotionally abusive relationships. Since I have witnessed Annie's clinical expertise as a skilled therapist, I marvel at her unwillingness to hide behind her role in this book. She uses her own story, her own shame and pain, to help others see that they aren't the only ones that are caught in the emotional bondage of a failed relationship with a love avoidant partner.

Annie is willing, throughout the book, to model the humility that it takes to claim denial of the hurt and distortion of reality that comes with the idealized fantasies of romantic love. Annie brings the reality of Love Addiction to life in a very dramatic way, starting with her initial discovery that the man in her life was living a complete lie. She challenges the myth of romantic love that leaves so many open to manipulation and disappointment at the hands of a master con artist. Annie allows us to witness the torment and horror she feels as she uncovers the truth about his false promises and her shattered dreams along with the tall order that coming out of the Love Addicted trance means.

What I like about Annie Bennett's style is her willingness to take ownership of her own part in feeding an emotionally abusive relationship. She de-victimizes herself by seeing how she was set up for emotional abuse in her own family of origin, while experiencing the legitimate feelings of abandonment by her childhood family system. She shows by her own example that we can't recognize toxic people in adulthood if we idealize abusing caregivers in our childhood.

As Annie so graphically illustrates, emotional predators like her love avoidant partner, count on the reluctance of their victims to self-disclose. These emotional hostage-takers use their victim's shame to isolate them from outside intervention, starving them from nurturing relationships that could help free them. Too many people stagnate and die in emotionally draining relationships to avoid feeling shame and being shamed. Annie gives hope to those who still suffer. Readers will find solace in Annie's story, that 'I'm not the only one. If Annie can come out of hiding and ask for help, so can I.'

The Love Trap offers a path toward freedom from love addiction. Chapters 1 and 2 describe, in a daring way, the shock of hitting bottom. Annie Bennett takes us though her emotional carnage as the 'house of cards' collapses, as the addictive relationship disintegrates into the sham it always was, but which she couldn't see.

Later chapters take us on a journey into Annie's past where she traces the course of her own development towards Love Addiction. As she paints the picture of the typical childhood of a Love Addict, she highlights the limitations of her own parents, along with the reality of her abandonment as a little girl. She challenges her shame created by her family of origin and the powerful injunction, 'don't rock the boat'. Annie shows us the way – that the truth will set us free of parental idealization, which leaves Love Addicts open to predatory manipulation. She is a living example that no matter how well educated and capable, if the Love Addict can't recognize the dangers in the past, then she can't avoid the cloak of toxicity in present love interests. On the contrary, as Annie's experience shows us, she repeatedly ran back into the arms of disaster in a state of rapture, even in the face of futility and spiritual bankruptcy.

The book also gives practical tips on how to begin the recovery process. Annie shares her emergence into relationship competence with herself, her children and significant others. Fortunately, there is help available for taking these monumental steps towards liberation from Love Addiction. Annie outlines the way out that she took towards self-love and true empathy, especially with her own children. She highlights the signposts of evolving personhood through specific self-nurturing exercises that break the multigenerational, carried bonds of shame and victimization in families.

Annie Bennett is an example of what American psychotherapist Arnold Mindell (born 1940) calls 'deep democracy'. She allows her previously denied feelings of shame, sadness, fear and anger to participate in her decision to leave a debilitating love addictive relationship. Her effectiveness and modeling in claiming her feelings in the presence of loving witnesses serves as a beacon for those who read *The Love Trap* – calling them to their own freedom, not only socially but in the core of their inner lives.

Annie is a consummate 'wounded healer'. She inspires with her personal vulnerability as well as her professional expertise in the spirit of helping active Love Addicts who still cry alone in the night.

Kip Flock, MSW, LCSW, BCD
Former Clinical Director of the John Bradshaw Center
Los Angeles, California, USA

INTRODUCTION

Some people believe that addiction to love is fun, glamorous, exotic, and even erotic. They may think it is simply about experiencing love many times over. The truth, as with any other addictive behaviour, is quite different. I will show in this book how acutely painful and disruptive this addiction can be.

The book will guide you through an autobiographical journey of Love Addiction in action: this voyage offers you the opportunity to witness a powerful Love Addiction in progress and to experience it, vicariously, for yourself. The purpose of the story is to encourage you to recognise your own possible Love Addiction and, from that point, to enable the healing process to begin. The purpose of a personal disclosure is to provide a very detailed case study in order to analyse how the abnormal and unhealthy cycle of Love Addiction perpetuates itself. Accordingly, I hope you will gain wisdom and insight into your own cycle of behaviour.

Many good books have been written on the addictive interaction between the Love Addict and the 'Love Avoidant'. This book, however, focuses primarily on the Love Addict cycle and just briefly explains the attraction between the Love Addict and the Love Avoidant personality. It shows how the Love Addict uses denial, repeatedly, as a protective, coping mechanism and relies upon fantasy as the rescuing device.

Commitment phobia, similar to Love Avoidance, is an anxiety state that can arrest and sabotage relationships. Anxiety, or fear, is the chief mood state experienced by the Love Avoidant: the fear associated with being too emotionally close and the threat of emotional suffocation. Such fear can present with physical symptoms, such as panic attack, affecting the body in a number of different ways.

For the purposes of this book, I refer to the Love Avoidant as He and the Love Addict as She. However, both men and women can experience either of the two states and people can swing between Love Addict and Love Avoidant within the same relationship and within different relationships.

It is unsurprising that both emotional states can occur within one person. The primal or earliest relating pattern, in childhood relationships, is key to the destructive patterns we adopt. These are immaturity issues that were not resolved during childhood and adolescence. When stuck deep within the pain of not having basic love and attention needs met at the most important stage of emotional development, the adult may, subconsciously, attempt to resolve that pain by recreating a dysfunctional attachment.

Hostage to misery and pain

If you recognise that you have a repetitive pattern of behaviour within your love relationships, which is keeping you hostage to misery and emotional pain, this book has been written for you. Any pattern or habitual behaviour can lead to compulsion and progressively into addiction: in other words, a compelling need to repeat. I will show you the processes of Love Addict behaviour, and why and how these processes have unfolded. You will become aware of the choices you have been making which have trapped you deep within emotional love despair. The information in this book will offer you a simple and easy to understand way of recovering from the misery and heartbreak that result from a compulsive and addictive cycle.

Watching out for patterns

First, ask yourself if you repeat relationship cycles. Do you always choose the wrong man or the wrong woman? Take the time to examine your history of love relationships, from your teens onwards, using this book as your guide.

Many people want the answers without asking the relevant questions. As you have chosen this book, you are already on the way to determining the relevant questions: the questions you need to ask in order to formulate your answers and resolve your emotional conflicts.

Recovery comes more easily when we apply sense and logic to what may seem, at first, like a senseless situation. Look for signs of patterns playing out. Patterns are established by learning something in a certain way, while repetition makes those patterns stick and reinforces the message. Rather like a pumped up muscle, the more it is flexed the stronger and more powerful it becomes. Repetition and intensity make our patterns progressive. Addictions are progressive, compulsive behaviours and thoughts that build into an unmanageable, dysfunctional energy force. Dysfunction is the inability to function normally or deal with social relations in a balanced, healthy way. The process of Love Addiction, like all other addictions, proves with time to be destructive and painful.

Reality of the love relationship

Time and time again, my clients tell me, 'If only he would see that he doesn't have to do this. We were so happy. I don't want to hurt him or be too demanding of him; I can do things for myself', 'We were so good together, just the other day he told me he loved me, we were close'. The Love Avoidant is likely to fear that too much is being expected of him and to fear that he risks losing his identity, his self. The Love Addict misses the point that the complaint has nothing to do with the reality of the relationship. It reflects the anxiety experienced by the Love Avoidant, which is stimulated by relating with the Love Addict. When the Love Addict begins to withdraw, feeling hurt and abandoned, and the Love Avoidant consequently no longer feels he is suffocating, he may well feel safe enough to re-enter the relationship.

Denial of what is really happening in a relationship is perhaps the hardest issue to overcome for the Love Addict; it certainly is the biggest obstacle to recovery. Denial is likely to have been used as a coping, protective mechanism against what appeared to be an unacceptable experience, piece of information or behaviour. The pain and damage that Love Addiction can cause, not only at an emotional level but also at a physical level, will become clear; my hope is that the information within this book will help prevent people creating more 'mistaken identities' – in other words, relationships based on denial and fantasy, withdrawal and hurt. My intention is to enable those of us who have suffered the failure of relationship after relationship to find the solutions to such dysfunctional relationship cycles and enable each one of us to adopt the necessary measures to prevent further heartache and the bitter destruction of relationships.

Learning to trust in real love

How do we know if we are experiencing true, real love? Do we trust our sense of euphoria? Do we measure it by our physical sense of elation? Or do we rely upon our long-term judgment? Many relationships begin with an overwhelming sensation of euphoria, the look in the eyes, the touch of that person, the smell of their presence, the sense of humour, the laugh, the voice. These are some of the signs that stir our emotions and alert us to something special. Other signs may include the intellectual stimulation from the other person or their perceived kindness and caring, leading us to feel appreciated, valued and loved.

The rush of adrenaline that we experience when we are in contact with or even just thinking about that special person can be seductive and addictive. We feel good when we are immersed in those thoughts or in the company of that person. This feeling is not necessarily experienced from one relationship to another in multiple styles; it can be felt and experienced within one long-term relationship. To continue such a cycle within a relationship that is not based in reality offers no actual security and is ultimately exhausting. A sense of closeness followed by withdrawal and then back to closeness again can become the regime within the relationship, creating a rollercoaster, swinging pattern of behaviour.

The Love Addict makes her partner or spouse her drug of use. To the Love Addict a relationship can be similar to a stash of drugs to a substance addict or alcohol to an alcoholic. The addict ultimately hands over her own personal power to the drug and places it in a position of higher power than her own self. Withdrawal is often a physically painful and emotionally agonising experience with effects similar to a heroin addict going cold turkey. The Love Addict enters a trance-like state, hypnotised by her love partner, and to be separated from the relationship represents a painful withdrawal. The compulsion to continue with the relationship is overwhelming and devastatingly destructive, with real physical withdrawal symptoms.

The effects often extend beyond the Love Addict into her wider relationships, thus causing disturbance to family, friends and work colleagues. The devastation through divorce, for example, can induce all sorts of emotional and physical symptoms of stress, both to the two parties and to relatives and friends. Obsessive thought about the love partner can lead to destructive acts, fuelled by anger at the perceived desertion and cruelty by the former partner, occasionally leading to murder, *le crime passionel*.

Radiant in new love

It is the feel-good endorphins that carry the messages around our body to let us know we are feeling love and want to pursue the relationship.

I see clients in my practice who experience a tremendous adrenaline rush in the first period of their relationship. Entry into the new relationship is usually quick and intense, both for the Love Addict and the Love Avoidant.

It is widely understood that our feelings during the onset of a love relationship are greatly influenced by the chemical changes we experience, which we interpret as emotionally charged love feelings: the 'high' we get is similar to the high from any drug or mood-altering experience and it lasts only into the initial emotional stage of the relationship. This is where the opportunity for healthy relating begins. This is also where many people suffering from relationship compulsivity (the need to repeat) or addiction tend to leave the relationship or create withdrawal from the relationship in order to experience the rush of intensity when the relationship gets back together. This is because the heady rush no longer exists in the second stage and the inclination to be in a relationship declines, rather like coming down from a mood-enhancing drug.

The 'want' is very different to the 'desire'. Desire is the drive that craves the drug, the search for ecstasy. The want is a choice we make about something that we consider in an objective and rational way, using moderation as a guideline, relying upon a sense of what is useful and nurturing to us. An alcoholic in recovery may tell you that he doesn't even like the taste of alcohol and a sex addict will admit when he is in recovery that it is not the enjoyment of sex that creates the strongest drive. Clearly, the want is not the drive towards the compulsion or repetition: it is the desire, the search for his or her own sense of ecstasy.

Swept away

The power of desire has the capacity to ruin people and nations. Think of the many politicians that have been brought down by their emotional and sexual desires. Consider the impact that has upon a nation, with its capacity to leave an entire political party in despair. Take, as an example, Bill Clinton, who transfixed the world with his vision and representation of the truth in order to protect himself from the consequences of his sexual activities. An intelligent and admirable world-class leader's career was threatened by his emotional and sexual pursuits.

We see many examples, particularly in show business and the music industry, of marriages that are made too quickly and self-destruct with the agonising details of private lives and financial issues being splashed across tabloid newspapers. And, often, there may be a young child at the centre of the storm who takes on the burden of emotional conflict and anger within the home. Such marriages act as a clear warning sign to anyone about to enter a serious and binding commitment of the need to gather information from a cross-section of the new partner's close friends and family. Whirlwind love relationships can leave the new baby or child set up for a future of repeating her parents' love relationship. The financial consequences of Love Addiction may add to the intensity and fury of the break-up, making it even more difficult to reach an amicable divorce settlement, which would enable the family to move forward towards a sound and stable future. Deep-seated anger and resentment can keep a relationship actively engaged, in a negative way, as it journeys through the grief and disappointment that the dreams it once represented have so swiftly disappeared. Never mind the fact that friends may have predicted an obvious incompatibility and a disastrous outcome.

What stirs us into real love or the sense of feeling good about ourselves? The answer lies in the information that is stored in the areas of the brain known as the amygdala and the hippocampus, responsible for emotion and memory. Our early life experiences create the template that forms future relationships. The template is our early developmental framework, which shapes our thinking and behaviour patterns. If we take this information and relate it to the amount of energy – which may be defined as the attention and time invested by one person in another – that is directed by the child to the major caregivers (usually, the parents), we may be able to trace a pattern of self-defeating behaviours, caused by an imbalance in the energy expended by each party.

The repetitive quest leading to Love Avoidance

Ask yourself if an extraordinary amount of your energy was given to your parental figure, or major caregiver, when you were a child. A major caregiver is anyone that had a significant part to play in your upbringing. It may have been a parent, grandparent, teacher, babysitter/nanny or an elder sibling. If we connect the level of energy to the experience of the memory and emotion centre of the brain, we may determine what style of relationship has been created and is likely to be recreated in the future with adult relationships. For example, the child that has tried endlessly, in vain, to win appropriate love and attention from his mother can only keep trying. But she demands more and more of his attention by means of helping her in the house, by running to the shops, by watching over younger siblings or by having to listen to her talk about her relationship problems. The child makes an endless, fruitless, effort to receive the love he deserves and wants. Alas, appropriate love is not returned and he soon picks up the message that to love is to serve or care take. Love becomes a duty and, in return, even more is expected – and again he gives, in the hope that one day love will be shown to him.

Trying to win love in this way is a self-defeating cycle and resentment builds, as the child never actually receives what he wants and needs in the way of love and attention. He learns how he functions in important relationships: he interprets his experience as a need to give. He does the giving and she does the taking. He has learned to interpret his role in love relationships (an example of how children adapt to their environment in an attempt to have their needs and wants met). He learns to avoid love relationships as a means of self-protection, in other words, to be Love Avoidant. This is usually the style of relationship that hooks the Love Addict.

Love Addiction may be triggered by early experiences of rejection and abandonment. The child may interpret this as a loss, of feeling that there is something wrong, ugly or nasty about her and that is why she is unlovable. When a love partner arrives on the scene and clearly signals to her her value – because now, apparently, she is important enough to have time and energy spent on her – the Love Addict is joyous. The search for true love need go on no longer, the other person (the Love Avoidant) has personified the perfect love role model. The Love Addict may appear to sit back on her laurels and expect an ever-flowing river of attention and care. It is an innocent stance that reveals the inner child acting out her unresolved loss and grief for what was expected as her due in childhood but not received.

The Love Addict appears to need taking care of; she appears vulnerable, soft, gentle, loving: everything the Love Avoidant could wish for in order to prove his worth. In reality, she may be strong, successful and independent. The stimuli acted upon by the Love Avoidant allow the fantasy to act as a propellant from Love Avoidant to Love Addict: he is the knight in shining armour or she is the superwoman, the higher power and pseudo parent.

Hope within the Love Addiction fantasy

A client in therapy, expressing the profound distress felt by her inner child in search of love and attention, wrote this fairytale of Love Addiction:

Once upon a time there was a young girl called Tina. She lived in a big, big house in the middle of nowhere. She spent her days dreaming of the man who was going to save her from her life. This man would be handsome, charming and confident. He would come to sweep her off her feet and love her so much that all the pain she had ever felt in the world would disappear.

Tina did meet this man, time and time again, but each one always left her once he got to know her. This made her pain more real and moved it closer to her heart. This deepened pain made the man who would eventually come and save her seem further and further away. When she was with one of these men, it was always perfect to begin with, and she felt deliriously happy. It would not have been possible for anyone to feel happier. Nothing could touch her, as she was invisible. But, slowly, the uneasy, panicky feeling would set in, at around the same time that the man's interest was starting to waver. Tina would be so desperate to cling on to the happiness and so scared of being left alone that she would try to guess what the man wanted. Then she would become that girl [the girl she guessed the man wanted]: but the more she did this, the less interest he showed in her. This made her hurt so much, all over, that she wanted to die.

Eventually, these men, one by one, would leave her; most of them wouldn't even say goodbye and she would be left wondering what she did wrong and what it was about her that made them want to leave her. She would feel ashamed that she wasn't good enough for these men and that she wasn't even worth saving.

Occasionally, a good, decent man would come along, a man who would make her feel safe and content and everything in her body would be calm and settled. But not one could save her, for they could not reach her. Tina preferred to spend her time and energy with the men who made her feel sad and uneasy: for the few times she was winning, it was the greatest feeling in the world. But this feeling was very short lived and then, once again, she began to repeat the painful cycle.

One day Tina woke up and decided that she wanted to change her life, for it occurred to her that maybe it wasn't just bad luck, and perhaps it was something in her behaviour that created the same pattern again and again.

Tina went to see her fairy godmother who would teach her how to change her life. She was very scared at the thought of changing and her feelings for each of these men were still so strong she was sure she could never break free. But, for the first time ever, she could see clearly that the man for whom she had been waiting her whole life, the man who was to save her, didn't exist at all. And, instead of feeling sad, Tina felt hopeful.

(Quoted with permission)

Learning to enjoy real love

Love is much more than the early euphoria; it is long-term companionship and support for each other that extend beyond the early stages of a love relationship. As men and women grow older, perhaps around the fifty-year mark, the levels of the sex hormones in the body change. Oestrogen levels decline, and the biological urge lessens. Testosterone levels become reduced and less demanding. Relationships at this time have an opportunity to plateau, allowing them to become more mellow and more confident without being propelled by the important sex hormones that drive procreation.

A slow start to relationships enables us to check what's going on between each other, to be thoughtful, and to apply commonsense when it is needed. A slow start demonstrates an ability to use the 'want' within us, allowing each partner to understand that s/he is a worthy and balanced partner with whom to be in love. If dysfunction has been the template or foundation for a person's upbringing (with these early experiences showing the child how to behave and think), such dysfunction may play itself out later in close adult relationships. It is possible to have a love-addicted relationship with people other than the main love focus, for example, with a sibling, a son or daughter, or a work colleague or boss. An important element within the Love Addiction cycle is the trance-like state mentioned earlier, in which the relationship partner is promoted as the higher power, with the Love Addict ignoring signs, facts and reason.

Dysfunctional childhood experiences do not necessarily result in dysfunctional adult relationships. Many relationships can function perfectly well, and in balance, even if both partners have experienced an emotionally unhealthy or damaged early childhood. However, for the purposes of those suffering and struggling with Love Addiction, I will focus on dysfunctional, repetitive behaviours that have caused distress within relationships. This book is designed to help you gain relief and insight into relationship stresses. You may decide to take your journey of exploration further, in conjunction with this book, through therapy or counselling (via your family doctor) in order to find a way to understand the patterns and compulsions (repetitions) that lead to a dysfunctional relationship.

My personal experience of Love Addiction

As an example of the depth of destruction that dysfunctional relationships can cause, I have written of my personal experience. This relationship unfolded over the course of six very intense and highly charged months of my life. 'Trauma bonding', which is described in Chapter 5, *The burden of shame*, was stimulated by the legal battle I felt I had to fight in order to provide for and to protect my children. This most vulnerable time allowed the door to be opened to my knight in shining armour.

Thus began my journey through a fantasy, love-addicted relationship. This is my true story (though names and other details have been changed to maintain the privacy of others) and the subsequent chapters offer an outline of how to find psychological relief from dysfunction within intimate relationships between two people. The other relationships in your life may also benefit from understanding the processes of Love Addiction and Love Avoidance.

For the purposes of analysis and exploration I refer to myself as Alice Brooks: although this is a personal disclosure, I have found a pseudonym makes it easier to take an objective view. The characters in my disclosure have also been renamed to assure anonymity. I also tell my story from a completely personal point of view – the behaviour of other people, including my ex-husband, may have appeared quite different to others and motives may have been quite different to what I supposed; what is important for understanding Love Addiction is my subjective experience as a Love Addict. I tell the story of my experience in the form of an autobiographical novel, in order to offer you an opportunity to explore an extreme case of Love Addiction and its consequences, together with analytical feedback at each stage of the journey.

I offer you my personal view of life at the time, together with my professional analytical commentary. The initial stages of my recovery involved writing about my experience as a means of processing the pain, and I offer this to you as a tool for your own recovery, a reference from which you may explore, learn and develop.

Chapter
1

A Case of Mistaken Identity

England, December

'Good morning, Belgian Embassy.'

'Hello. May I speak to the Ambassador, please?'

'This is the emergency telephone number. Is it urgent?' the voice on the other end said.

'Well, yes, I think so. Is he there?'

'No, this number is only for emergencies.' The voice sounded rather short and disgruntled.

'I'll call back.' I hung up, feeling exhausted and weary.

An hour later I tried again.

'Hello. May I speak to the Ambassador, please?'

'Who's calling?'

'My name is Alice Brooks. I am the fiancée of Charles Bertrand.'

'Hello. This is the Ambassador of Belgium speaking. How can I help?' His voice was calm and gentle.

'Hello. My name is Alice Brooks and I am the fiancée of Charles. I am sorry to tell you that Charles passed away in the early hours of this morning.' I was relieved to pass the information on to Charles's friend and country representative.

'Who is Charles?' he said.

'Charles Bertrand.' I thought perhaps he hadn't heard me properly the first time.

'I am sorry. I do not know a Charles Bertrand. I am sorry to hear of your loss. Is there anything I can do?' His voice was concerned and kind. He could obviously hear my anxiety.

'Oh, no. I'm sorry to trouble you. You don't know Charles?' I had to check it.

'No. Is he Belgian?' he enquired.

'Yes, he was. I'm sorry to trouble you. Goodbye.' I replaced the receiver.

It was then that my tragedy turned into a nightmare.

My overwhelming sense of shock had left me almost paralyzed. I was incapable of thinking straight. I struggled to make any sort of sense of the events of the past forty-eight hours…and the last six months.

Charles had told me that he was a close friend of the Belgian Ambassador. The Ambassador's wife came from Liverpool and they often spent evenings discussing foreign affairs over a glass of wine. Once he brought back home a bottle of wine or two, a gift from the Ambassador himself. I couldn't understand. How could the Ambassador not know Charles? Andrea will know. I must contact Andrea.

Charles had told me that Andrea was his personal secretary, who had worked for him for twenty years, and dealt with all his affairs. She was based in Belgium and worked out of the same office as his daughter Marie, the Belgian court's Coroner. They also shared an office at his home in Belgium. I needed to find the telephone number for Andrea in order for her to help. There was so much to be done. The family needed to be informed and asked what they wanted to do with the body. Charles had wanted to be buried in Cornwall; would they mind? Would they be coming over?

I searched through Charles's belongings. It was one of the hardest things I had had to do. Tears kept falling; I could not believe that my dear beloved Charles was no longer here with me. He was the one that I could usually depend on and lean on in difficult times. I thought of him as my rock. I needed him.

I began to look through his diary. It started from 1 July. He had torn out all the previous pages. He told me his life had begun when he met me, on that day in July. That had been intensely flattering … and I had simply believed him.

THERAPEUTIC ANALYSIS: DENIAL AND FANTASY

The point at which denial is broken can be the most painful emotional stage of the Love Addiction cycle. It is when reality is forced upon us and the fantasy of the perfect relationship must be let go.

Fantasy is a mainstay of the Love Addiction disease. If you are a Love Addict, almost certainly it will have saved you in your formative years from the extraordinary emotional pain of rejection, abandonment, disapproval or non-acceptance by your major care giver, (probably one of your parents). I had built a strong fantasy based on very little reliable evidence from Charles.

Childhood experience of shocking rejection by my father had compelled me to protect my 'self' by fantasizing impossible and unrealistic relationships into reality. The more I was rejected, the more I wanted the other person to fulfil my need. In effect, this kept me setting myself up for failure and appearing needy. This is typical of the Love Addict, who tries in vain to avoid rejection and ensure acceptance and value through the partner. It is not so much a protection as a re-enactment. It keeps the Love Addict within the loop of: 'The fantasy of success – I've found the knight in shining armour who will now save me and truly love me – and give me my sense of value as a person'. Choosing partners who lived at a distance was a subtle way of setting the stage for manageable rejection and abandonment. This was a form of trauma re-enactment to manage the overwhelming emotional pain of disapproval and rejection from the damaged primary love relationship I had suffered as a child with my father. At that stage I had needed to develop a coping strategy with which I could manage the feelings of rejection and transcend the pain of disapproval.

Denial and fantasy are useful tools for the broken-hearted child. It is unfortunate that the child is likely to use these tools to survive into

adult love relationships, creating an inappropriate model for relating,
culminating in a self destructive and immature way of relating.

Had I have been able to think rationally, with a normal mindset,
I would have wondered why Charles's diary did not include the details
of his life before he had met me. My inner voice would have been ready
to ask questions, such as why had I never witnessed a conversation with
his PA or been more aware of his life in Belgium and his friends and col-
leagues. These were the sorts of questions that needed to be asked for my
own protection.

London, 1 July of the same year

I was a counselling therapist finishing my final studies in London. One of
my colleagues was having a party and had invited me to come along. I
wasn't sure if I would go, as I was not very keen on this particular person
from my group, Zhora. I decided to accept the invitation on the grounds
that I would be sure to find a friendly and sensitive side to Zhora. Well, it
proved to be true that she was different on her own territory.

I arrived late. The journey had taken me longer than I thought. I
took the Underground from central London all the way out to a distant
part of North London, some hour and twenty minutes. Stuck in a hot and
sweaty train, wearing an exotic, velvet designer evening suit, I felt ridicu-
lously over dressed for the journey.

When I arrived the room was full of people from different countries:
Greeks, Italians, Belgians, Iranians, Jamaicans and English. It was a cul-
tural spectacular. Zhora had cooked for an army and set out the table for
all to help themselves. She introduced me to her group of friends: Tony,
the Italian hairdresser; Sarah, the lawyer; Grace, another therapist; and
Charles, the Belgian Supreme Court Judge. I was happy to chat and get
acquainted with each of them. They all seemed very pleasant people.
Charles began to talk to me about his time in England and how he had
taken time off from his duties to have a sabbatical. He was charming and
invited me to the launch of a new restaurant in London. I said I would

think about it and see if I was able to make it. I gave him my telephone number so that he could confirm whether or not I was going to be there.

The rest of the evening was spent dancing, eating and chatting with all the different people around the room. It was a successful party. Nobody got drunk and it was all very enjoyable and lively with plenty of laughter.

The following day Charles telephoned me and seemed eager that I should go to the opening of the new restaurant. He was overseeing the opening himself. I was flattered at his insistence and gracefully accepted.

We met in London at the launch. The place was full of people who I did not know. This was a prospect that I enjoyed: new place, new people, what fun.

A gentleman met me at the door. His job was to act as host to the crowd and make sure that everyone mingled. He passed me a glass of champagne and introduced me to a small group of people and then politely left to continue with his mission.

'Have you met Charles?' one of the group said. 'He is a Supreme Court Judge. And the chairman of this private club along with many other enterprising business interests.'

'Yes, thank you. We met the other evening, although Charles did not tell me about all his exploits.' Then I continued,

'How interesting for you,' as I turned to look at Charles.

Our eyes met and he began to tell me of his exciting life. He was on a seven-year sabbatical from Belgium. The last case he had worked on had been very high profile and he informed me that he had had to leave his country for a period of time for his own safety.

I was suitably impressed and intrigued. I listened intently to what he said, mesmerised by his story. He told of long lasting friendships with royalty, particularly the King of Spain, for whom he ran special missions. Of friendships with landed gentry, not to mention the close contact he had with MI6 and the security services. I was transfixed and intensely flattered that he would tell me his story. He told me of the near miss he had had while working as a Supreme Court Judge in Madrid. Someone from the Ministry of the Interior, he claimed, had been sent to lay him down (his expression: it meant to get him out of the picture, kill him). They allegedly had taken a shot at him and only just missed his head. He showed me the mark where the bullet had skimmed across his forehead.

I was overawed – and deeply fascinated. There was actually a scar that supported his claim.

That evening was an evening never to forget. The energy between our eyes expressed a deep sense of knowing and excitement, as if we were soulmates joined together again. Sparks were flying and my heart skipped a beat. I felt as though I could see deep inside his soul. My instinct was telling me loud and clear this man deserved love. He surely did, and I felt that I was the one to nurture him in it. His eyes were sea-green pools set in the clear white of innocence. His exuberance was remarkable. Nobody could ever forget meeting Charles. He had an extraordinary energy about him and a delightfully seductive accent. He stood about 6ft tall, distinguished looking with a cuddly, round middle, which made him even more lovable. I could identify with the child inside this wonderful, larger than life man. He was for me.

Later that night Charles asked if he might call me again to make a date. Happily, I said yes. I couldn't wait to hear more about his high profile missions and dangerous lifestyle.

It was not long before the call came. It was the following morning. I was finishing drying my hair and listening to some music. The phone rang and I picked up the receiver, while hurrying to turn the volume down on the radio.

'Hello,' I said.

'Hello, it's Charles Bertrand. I trust you are well? Would you like to come for dinner? Perhaps Thursday?' His voice was strong and direct.

I was surprised at the speed with which he had called me and by his prompt invitation. But I didn't hesitate.

'I'd love to. Where and at what time?' I replied.

He invited me to his home and explained that he was having the whole of the upper part of his residence repaired and redecorated as he had wound up his Chambers, which had been located in the building. There were some 40,000 books in storage boxes, the whole top part of the building needed refurbishment, and so we would have to make do with the basement for the time being. He told me that there were staff finishing off the process and they were on the next floor. He informed me that Catherine, who was his pupil barrister, was often doing legal work there. I did not mind in the least. I had been introduced by friends to Charles as a Supreme Court Judge, so I thought it would be perfectly safe to have dinner in his private residence. He gave me his telephone number in case of any problems and said goodbye.

It was later that night I realised that Thursday did present a problem. I had a prior engagement that had slipped my mind in the excitement. The following morning Charles called me again to say he had been called away on business and that we would have to rearrange our date. We rescheduled for the following day, Friday. I was relieved that Charles had changed the date, as I didn't want him to think that I would let him down. The following Thursday morning I had another call from Charles, telling me that he had managed to catch a ride in his friend's helicopter from the north of England and that he could make it after all if I was still available.

I was truly impressed. I really wanted to see him, so I cancelled my previous arrangement and made fresh plans with Charles.

I arrived at the front door bearing a beautiful bouquet of lilies. It seemed appropriate in the circumstances. After all, he was preparing dinner and entertaining me and I wanted to make an impression on him. I had come from work and so I needed to freshen up. I had brought the necessary things with me; Charles had invited me to stay over, as I had to be in central London early the next day. He showed me to the bathroom.

I wore lilac. It was warm and balmy that evening, so I needed no heavy clothing. Just a simple top and skirt. Charles was wearing a suit. He was impeccably dressed; something I would learn was quite usual for him.

He prepared a dinner of chicken in a white wine sauce with new potatoes and fresh vegetables. No wine was served. He had made it clear that he didn't want to spoil the occasion by drinking wine and not experiencing the 'truth of the evening'. I was surprised, but, nonetheless, respected his quirky behaviour and in a way enjoyed the evening even more because of it.

The rain began to fall. The air became heavy and stormy. Sultry. The light was spectacular, the kind of light one sees with the use of candles, perhaps in a church or darkened room. We heard the crack of thunder and wandered outside into the garden to see the beauty of the sky. It was a wonderful sight. With a dramatic clap of thunder, I felt protected and safe with Charles near me. We went back into to the dining room and sat opposite each other, glancing at one another as we talked.

The conversation was extraordinary. It began by Charles asking about my work and what it entailed. I am a counselling therapist and work in an integrative way. I explained that sometimes I found it useful to bring crystals and stones into a session for the use of emotional identification, that is to help enable a person identify those feelings that may be blocked off, repressed or difficult to express and to begin exploring their emotional world. Charles was intrigued and told me that he too had a crystal that he used for positive energy. He found it and put it on the table. I had brought my crystals with me as I had come from work and put them on display for him.

At this time Charles got out his tarot cards, which he said he had been taught in Spain during his time there, while he had studied law in Madrid.

The scene was exceptional. The sultry light, the thunder, the crystals, the magic between us and now Charles was going to read the tarot cards. I was totally swept away with the mood. He asked me to choose seven cards. They each held a significance for my future and my past. He told me of things that certainly rang true to my history and then he told me of things that were to happen in the future. Our relationship and love, our engagement, were among them. I was surprised at all this information coming so quickly at the very start of our relationship. However, my previous experience with the tarot had sometimes been surprisingly accurate, so I was confident of his reading. Charles exuded knowledge and self-assurance. We discussed the reading together with joint interest and amazement. We both could sense there was an electricity between us. But was this true? Were we destined for each other?

I was shocked and nearly speechless, but this was not a problem as

Charles spoke with such knowledge, interest and passion about so many things. My silence was unnoticed. The stories of his life were full and interesting. My life was full but his was packed with high profile, dangerous and important missions. He told me of one incident when he was shot in the leg. Naturally, I asked him why.

'I am a Supreme Court Judge. What do you think?' he snapped.

Well, I assumed there was a level of danger about such a position and Charles spoke with such authority. I dared not challenge him too much for fear of showing disbelief, which I thought would not be constructive. He showed me his paintings of landed gentry friends. The canvases were huge and the paintings were quite good. One in particular of a woman, a nude portrayed in a very natural way, took my interest.

Charles told me how his mother had been unable to breastfeed him as she had had no nipples. He said he had always been disappointed about this. This was unusual and underlined my initial instincts about his needing love and having an extraordinary energy with women.

The painting showed me that Charles had an interesting past in terms of relating to women. So much about him was interesting.

More and more I was falling in love. I had always seemed to need to be needed and I was loving every moment of it. Charles's qualities of mystery, intellect and excitement were perfect for my needs. My head was spinning.

Charles showed me to the spare bedroom. He kissed me gently and said goodnight. I lay on the bed, my mind swirling with soft, sweet loving thoughts, as happy as I could be, intoxicated by him.

Later, during the night I heard Charles enter the bedroom. I did not say anything, as deep down I wanted him. He came into the bed and moved beside me, his arm touching my side. I stirred and kissed his shoulder. He held me and kissed my hair. It was not long before Charles was enjoying the touch of my skin. He was all over my body, kissing me and touching me. I groaned with pleasure. My body was aching with desire as I kissed him back. We were entwined and loving every minute of it. I felt sure we were truly matched. Nothing could take this moment away; it was bliss.

Charles held me all night long, telling me that he loved me. It was too soon for me to tell him that I loved him, but my body and eyes would tell him. He covered my body with tiny kisses and we fell asleep.

In the morning we spoke of our plans for that day and the coming weekend. It was agreed that Charles would call me over the weekend.

Later, I met up with a couple of friends for lunch. I could not stop telling them about my experience. It was still overwhelming me. They listened and found it all totally fascinating. I was in a joyous world for the rest of the weekend. I hoped I would be for the rest of my life.

It would be the following Thursday before I heard from Charles again. The preceding week had been a tense blur of anticipation. I had been expecting his call since the weekend but I decided not to stress about it. After all, we were destined to be together, so the tarot said. My thoughts had begun to consider the possibility that maybe I had been mistaken. Maybe Charles had simply taken advantage of my trusting nature, but surely not. He was such a high profile person in such an important position, surely that couldn't be an option? I decided to trust myself and my intuition.

His call arrived. 'I have been away on business, in Bolton. I am the managing director of a paint manufacturing company there. I thought it best to give you some time to think. Would you like to join me for supper tomorrow evening? You may stay if you wish?'

I was again taken aback by his directness and speed.

'I have been thinking, Charles, and, yes, I would love to join you for supper,' I replied. 'About 7 p.m.?'

It was set, the time and the date. I was a little nervous. After all, it had been almost an entire week before he had called me. I kept reassuring myself, 'He is a busy man. Of course, he is with all the people he knows and he has many business interests.' I went to bed, thinking of what to wear and what our time would be like together after a week apart.

During the next day, my work colleagues asked me what the evening had been like the previous week. I told them that I had met the most extraordinary man. With all my heart I knew this and I told them that I was to meet with him later that day. They were so pleased for me. They had known me for some years. They believed it was rare for me to fall so deeply and so quickly for a man, although it would not be rare for a Love Addict, in fact. I had met many men but none had managed to claim my heart in such an intense, magnetic way in recent years.

I drove to London and approached Charles's residence. He stood outside, somehow knowing that I was near. He looked smartly dressed and I was thrilled to see him again. The look he gave me was matched by my feelings.

He gently kissed me on the cheek and ushered me into the basement again. Apparently, there had been many problems with the building works at his home, including rising damp. This time Charles had had oysters brought up to London from Cornwall especially for the occasion. He opened a bottle of Chablis and we enjoyed our supper. The evening passed sweetly, almost as if we had always been together. As though we had never been parted. It was so wonderful to be with him. His stories flowed like the wine and before we knew it we were in the bedroom making love with sensitivity and passion. We were fused together as though we had never been apart.

It was the following week that I was due to go to Spain and spend the summer with my family. The time would be long – a whole month before we would be together again. I did not want to seem too keen but secretly I yearned to tell him that I could be back sooner. He sensed the sadness of our separation but was certain that I should not upset my plans for the family summer. (My family consists of my two sons, Patrick, then fifteen, and Joseph, fourteen. Both the boys were attending a boarding school and were due to break up for the summer vacation.)

Charles was such a gentleman and I was proud of him for thinking of my family's disappointment at not having me with them for this time. He said he would take the opportunity to make the visit to Canada that he needed to make every year to check on operations in his banking business, and he promised to write.

THERAPEUTIC ANALYSIS: BOUNDARIES
Even at this early stage you can see how I entered the relationship without any boundaries. (These are the subject of Chapter 9: Recognising boundaries in relationships.)

First, I did not use any **listening boundaries**. I did not filter what was coming into my reality or check out any of the information I was receiving, though some of it was extraordinary. I took as truth everything Charles told me. A healthy listening boundary would have filtered data and asked for more information on subjects and issues that were unsubstantiated or hard to believe, ignoring the fact that it takes time to get to know another person.

I had learned that Charles was overseeing the opening of a restaurant, was a Supreme Court Judge in Belgium and Madrid, associated with MI6 and the Ambassador to Belgium, had a Rolls Royce and a property in Cornwall, a Spanish villa, a banking business in Canada, was the MD of a paint company in Bolton, chairman of a private club and, to cap it all, in danger of his life. The speed and the intensity of a Love Addiction can be so powerful that it will deceive the rational mind. When friends or family try to tell the Love Addict that they need to be careful and take a reality check, like any other addict, they are fiercely protective of their addiction and will not listen or, worse, do not hear. I could see that Charles was a very intelligent man. I had seen him speaking Spanish, French, Afrikaans and English. He certainly had a good knowledge of legal matters; indeed, he told me about the differences between Roman law and British law.

All in all, The Love Addict will overlook a very great deal – and suspend her critical faculties – in order to live out the fantasy and become alive. When we bypass our critical faculties, we enter a subconscious, entranced state in which information can seep into the psyche.

Second, I did not limit or restrain myself with a **talking boundary**. I opened up far too much, allowing my personal and private details to be disclosed too early in the relationship.

And, third, I did not observe a **sexual boundary**. A healthy sexual boundary gives time to gain more information about a person, their sexual history and status, before we can feel secure enough to be intimate together.

These boundaries are important, vital safety mechanisms, but they can be damaged. When we experience trauma of great intensity, we typically adapt a trauma response. I have described various important *trauma responses in Chapter 5: The burden of shame, but, in summary, early experiences of abandonment and rejection had led me to adapt a trauma response that included 're-enactment' and 'trauma splitting'. Trauma splitting is a way of distancing oneself from what is really going on; it can cause excessive daydreaming and fantasising, among other behaviours. I was picking up – without questioning – the fantasy that Charles spun as part of his seduction. Re-enactment led me to search endlessly for the complete love relationship I had never had. As a Love Addict I was drawn to important and powerful men, reflecting the way in which a child may perceive her father, in the hope they could save me from my emotional pain. Ultimately, I believed I would be rescued.*

If I had been relating in a healthy way, I would have recognised that it takes time to build trust. I would have made sure I gained additional information, would have held back on giving away too much about myself too quickly, and I would have given time for us to share personal feelings with sensitivity and appropriateness. But, for the Love Addict, the speed and intensity of development within a new relationship hook the trauma response. Charles was both speedy and intense and this behaviour speared me on his hook.

Spain, August of the same year

I went to Spain and waited for love letters from Charles.

He wrote. The news was sad, as a longstanding friend of his, whom he greatly admired, had died. He was going to the funeral and then there would be a memorial service. He sent me newspaper cuttings of the obituary and a glamorous photograph that was pictured alongside the wonderful words in her memory. Charles had been connected with her through joint business ventures in private clubs around London.

It was a while before I received another letter from Charles. I was surprised and disappointed. Then one day he called me. It was early in the morning. He told me he was calling from Buffalo, in the States. It was lovely to hear his soft voice and I was flattered that he would call me during a business trip. We exchanged our stories of the previous few weeks and 'kissed' each other down the telephone.

The month sped by with much anticipation of our reunion, I had told my mother and sisters about this wonderful larger than life man who had so certainly and colourfully entered my life. They were intrigued and eager to meet him. The end of August arrived, long awaited with anticipation and excitement.

Charles had asked that I call him the minute I arrived back at my apartment no matter what time it was.

London, late summer

It was 1.00 am but I called him. He was delighted and said that he would catch the early train to visit me. I took down the times of the trains and fell into a deep sleep.

The telephone rang – it woke me. 'Hello, Alice. It's Charles. I'm here at the railway station, I will be with you shortly,' he said. I ran around trying to tidy the apartment as the night before I had left suitcases and bags everywhere. The place was a mess. What would he think?

The doorbell rang – I was wearing nothing but my robe. Charles came into the room. It was sheer bliss to see him after all this time. He held me in his arms and kissed me tenderly. We looked at each other adoringly and talked about our time apart and how it had been difficult to imagine that we had been apart for so long. Never again, we both vowed. Charles drew me to the bedroom and laid me down on the bed. I was eager to make love with him once again, close together, never to be parted.

Later the next morning we set off for a walk in the park. The day was beautiful, the sun high in the sky. The park was magnificent in its splendour. The trees were full and the grass lay soft beneath our feet. People were laughing and the mood was relaxed. We walked and talked holding hands. It was almost as if our hearts were beating to the same tune. I felt secure with him by my side, knowing, somehow, that it would be for the rest of our lives.

Charles had made arrangements back in London for the Sunday, something important he told me. I didn't question him. I never did. I was so happy to be back with him; we were made for each other.

I called Charles on the telephone late Sunday evening. He was rather short with me as he said he still had company – the Belgian Ambassador. They were drinking wine and discussing world affairs. The Ambassador wanted Charles's help with something. I rang off, feeling a little uncomfortable that I had disturbed him.

The following day Charles called me and explained that it had been an awkward situation. I said that I understood and that I should have thought before I called.

THERAPEUTIC ANALYSIS: DISTANCE

*During the month apart and the next stage of the relationship we can see that I turned Charles in my imagination into what I wanted him to be; I 'objectified' him. Thinking obsessively about everything he had told me and waiting for his phone calls and letters, I built up a fantasy that denied how rarely he contacted me or how he was using **distance** in our relationship. I was lost in a fog of fantasy.*

The use of distance in a relationship as a way of keeping it from being intimate is a very important sign that any Love Addict prone to daydreaming and fantasy, needs to be aware of. The Love Addict's partner is often Love Avoidant, attracted by the Love Addict's need to be cared for but fearing intimacy and needing to gain a sense of relief from what may seem a suffocating relationship with the needy Love Addict.

As a Love Addict, you need to monitor how distance is being used in your relationship. True intimacy involves a mutual and respectful knowledge of the other person's qualities, their 'truth', without necessarily knowing every detail of their lives. It should be founded on mutual trust and emotional integrity. If we abandon our 'selves', we are vulnerable to endlessly objectifying and obsessing relationships. In Chapter 14: Taking care of yourself I look at how you can stay grounded in reality and not lose your sense of self.

London, September

Charles was due to come to visit me on his birthday and stay for a few days. I wanted so much to give him an experience that would be outstanding for him. I thought hard about the choices available. I didn't want just to take him out for dinner or lunch. That seemed so boring. I opted for something more romantic: a most beautiful location that opened its gates especially for the occasion. It was a botanical sculpture garden set in the Surrey countryside. The trees were turning from bright green to beautiful shades of gold and wine. The gardens showed off their unique beauty to the full, with innovative examples of modern sculpture. It was a first class choice to share a glorious birthday celebration.

I had put together a delicious picnic feast, with champagne and smoked salmon amongst other delicacies. The weather was beautiful and sunny, the perfect day; Charles was enchanted by the exceptional location, its isolation and tranquillity. He was impressed with the uniqueness of his birthday treat and I was happy that he was happy.

Our love and friendship were so natural and comfortable: it was simply meant to be.

Charles stayed with me for the week; I had wondered how he could manage to be away from his businesses for such a long time. When I questioned him about it, he replied that Andrea had everything under control and that she would email him should anything arise to concern him. This, I thought, was a sign of a truly well organised and successful man. Charles told me of his Rolls Royce, his chauffeur called Stefan. He kept the Rolls Royce in Cornwall away from the London hustle and bustle, not to mention theft and vandalism. I was really impressed with this. He told me it had cost him a great deal of money. One of the things I really liked about Charles was that, although he was obviously wealthy, he did not usually show it and gave the impression that it didn't matter to him. I was deeply impressed with this aspect of him and I loved the simplicity of our relationship, too. We would spend our time walking, talking, comforting and supporting each other. These were the things I held precious and dear.

Every evening would be a culinary delight. He preferred to eat in, while I cooked the most delicious meals for us, with loving tender care. We simply enjoyed being in the moment, each and every one.

THERAPEUTIC ANALYSIS: TAKING HOSTAGE

Here we can see that Charles was using money, or the pretence that he had plenty of it, as a way of keeping power within the relationship. I responded positively. For the Love Addict the all-powerful rescuer is a very important need.

At the same time, I had worked on the relationship in order to keep Charles close to me and secure his attention. In effect, I held him hostage within the relationship by making him feel special. Pleasing the partner excessively, keeping him comfortable without confronting him on issues that might be disturbing or worrying is a way of keeping the relationship going. It is a way of holding the other person hostage. Placing the partner on a pedestal creates a powerful position for him, or her, and not a position that he will be likely to want to give up. The effect is that he will become hostage to feeling powerful in the relation-ship. He may stay in the face of destruction to satisfy his need to be spe-cial until such time that strong emotions such as anger, fear and panic set in and a sense of suffocation takes over, overwhelming him, the Love Avoidant partner.

October

The surprise came one morning when I decided to check on the lateness of my period by taking a home pregnancy test. The result was positive. At first I found it difficult to believe. I had not even thought of more children and I found the prospect of a baby with the man I simply adored over-whelming. I was happy and joyful and so was Charles.

We walked to the town with our news and bought the latest books on pregnancy and spent the rest of the day reading about the fascinating miracle that lay ahead of us.

Charles was like a small child himself, so enchanted with the idea of having another child. He casually slipped into the conversation that we would shortly be engaged and married not long afterwards. This, he thought, would be a respectful way to introduce the newborn baby into the world, legitimately.

Charles had not asked me to marry him. He just assumed it by putting it to me this way. I was taken aback, but something rather agreeable came over me, too. He was so powerful and I loved that.

Our engagement was to be announced in December. Charles wanted to make sure that we were properly engaged before my pregnancy began to show and he began to introduce me to his family and friends. I was carried away with the excitement and future plans.

It was at about this time that I embarked upon a legal challenge to gain financial support to enable my sons to continue being privately educated. The strain I had been under to pay for their education had been immense. I had delayed this course of action for years, as I knew it would be traumatic for me to take on the other party. I was low on energy levels but my newfound love recharged my batteries sufficiently to take this action. My lawyer told me that I should have addressed this issue years before, but the trauma of all that was involved with going to court had stopped me. However, Charles managed to give me some good advice concerning this. He knew so much about the law and offered to research certain aspects and call friends who were specialists in family law as his own speciality was criminal law.

I received a phone call from Joseph one evening the following week, after he had spent the weekend with his father. He reported that things had not gone too well and his father had threatened to hit him and had pinned him up against the wall. Poor Joseph was terrified. I did my best to calm him and told him that I would collect him on Wednesday evening and bring him and his brother back to the apartment for supper where we would all discuss the matter in detail.

I explained to Charles what Joseph had told me had happened to him. He was in disbelief that such a thing could happen between a father and son. Charles was very supportive. He planned what we should have for dinner that night and insisted that he would cook while I fetched the boys from their school.

I brought Joseph and Patrick back home. We walked through the door to a wonderful aroma of chicken casserole that had been lovingly prepared by Charles. The boys were tight with stress. We managed to put off the conversation about the weekend until we were all seated around the table.

Joseph told his story and Patrick confirmed it. They both reported that their father had been violently threatening to Joseph. I asked the boys what they wanted me to do. Joseph said he never wanted to see his father again and Patrick echoed, 'I never want to speak to him either,' and so I asked them if they wished me to initiate legal action and they both replied with a firm yes.

I assured them I would go to the law courts the following morning and put the process in action, which I did. Charles echoed that this was a necessary step and that the law of the land was there to protect children in such circumstances.

This was not the first occasion that the boys had reported this type of pressure from their father. I felt it had to stop and was determined to protect them from him, as I saw it, once and for all.

I am sure that having the support and love from Charles gave me the strength to confront my ex-husband, something that I dreaded doing as he still held a position of fear over me. My experience of life with him had been abusive and now he appeared to me to be threatening to abuse our children. Overwhelming energy was needed for me to take this action and, without Charles's support, it would have been too much to bear.

I drove the boys back to school and reassured them that things would work out and it would be better soon, although the situation was tough right now.

First thing the next morning I applied to the courts for a restraining order. The legal wheels began to turn. I informed the school of the action I had taken and heard no reply. I assumed all was well, but I was wrong.

Charles had to return to London on the Friday, for an important meeting he had with the Belgian Ambassador over the weekend. It gave me an ideal opportunity to be with the boys alone.

Saturday morning the post arrived and in it was the legal documentation from the law courts, a copy to me and one to the boys' father. Sunday morning I received a telephone call from the Headmaster of the school, informing me that their father had been calling them. He was extremely angry and was demanding to see the boys. I explained that his visiting rights were for the following weekend and that we would cross that bridge when we reached it. The Headmaster asked to see the boys that evening for a private meeting. I agreed and that evening they went into his office. I left to return home, only to receive a telephone call from my ex-husband from the Headmaster's office. He had been at the meeting. I was astounded at the insensitivity I felt the Headmaster had shown in such a delicate matter, and the deceit I felt had been used to bring the father to face his children. In my view the school had put the alleged perpetrator in front of the victim, without my knowledge or prior notice to the boys. I was shocked and outraged at what seemed to me the lack of care shown by the school. I was sure both Joseph and Patrick had been traumatised.

I called Charles in London, my voice shaking with anger and fear, because I was convinced the boys were being psychologically damaged by events at the school.

'Hello, Charles. It's me. I can't believe what has just happened. It's terrible. Can you talk?' I quivered.

'No, I told you I was busy and I am. It is not convenient to talk now,' came Charles's reply.

The phone went down.

I was shocked at his cold and distant response, as he knew the importance of the situation. My anger was compounded by his response. I felt alone and let down, abandoned by Charles, and the school, powerless and desperate. I also felt betrayed by my children for apparently inviting their father to a meeting at the school, although commonsense told me that the boys had had nothing to do with the invitation to meet him. My emotions told me of a conspiracy.

In my view I was simply trying to protect them from abusive behaviour from their father. My thoughts were uncontrollable; my emotions had the better of me. I cried and cried inconsolably. I wanted to die. The only thing that held me together was the thought of the tiny soul forming inside my body.

The following morning the disbelief at Charles's response was beginning to dawn on me.

The telephone rang and I could see Charles's number come up on the display. I did not want to speak to him. He sickened me. He must have tried to call about six times. Eventually, I decided to pick up the phone.

'Hello. What do you want?' I said.

'Alice, forgive me. I was in a very important meeting at that time with the Ambassador.'

'What, at ten o'clock on a Sunday evening?' I enquired.

'Yes. He is a very busy man and that was the only time he could manage. He brought around a bottle of whisky. He had many questions about national security and needed my help and experience,' Charles pleaded.

I was weak with emotional overload and needed his kindness and help. I wanted to believe him. I wanted our future to be happy together. I wanted my fantasy. At that time, I was devastated by what I felt was a complete lack of support and consideration shown me by the boys' boarding school. I had sent my children there in the belief that they would be looked after. In my view I was trying to protect the boys from their father, someone who had I believed bullied me. I was not going to let him do the same to the boys. That morning, when Charles rang, I still felt betrayed and abandoned; I had depended on Charles.

The post arrived later that morning, a letter from the boys' school. I opened it. It was an outline of what the school called *in loco parentis*; basically, the Headmaster had put himself in temporary parental power and control. He stated that both Patrick and Joseph had decided they did not want to see either their father or mother during the months of the continuing legal issues. I was devastated. He was telling me that I did not have the right to see or speak with my children for the following months until legal issues had been sorted. More devastating than anything was that he suggested the boys had requested this action. I broke down in disbelief. I asked myself, how could an institution that professed to look after its pupils take such a biased and uncaring standpoint. Surely it was clear that I was following the legal guidelines and that my only concern was to protect the children.

I cried until I hurt inside. I felt completely abandoned.

Charles arrived shortly after. He tried to assure me that this was a legal move that protected the children. I found it difficult to believe that he was so 'unemotional ' and detached. But once again I put my faith in his knowledge, despite the fact that some of my friends and colleagues were urging me to remove the boys from the school immediately.

Inside, the aching did not dissipate. Joseph was to celebrate his birthday soon. What was to happen? Was I not to see him or speak to him?

Charles assured me convincingly that my best position was to abide by the Headmaster's wishes. It would help in the forthcoming court appearance with regard to protecting the boys from my ex-husband's alleged aggressive behaviour. This felt like one of the most unnatural things that I had ever done. To this day I deeply regret it.

The day of Joseph's birthday came. I had bought a big birthday cake and vast quantities of Coca Cola for his dorm mates to enjoy. I wrapped his present and took it to the school, mindful that I did not have permission to see or speak to him. My heart broke. It felt so alien to be doing this. I wanted to hold Joseph in my arms and reassure him that everything was all right. I wanted to do the same with Patrick. I could not believe that they had requested a no contact rule.

The following weekend my family had a leaving celebration party for my sister and her husband. They were taking a travelling sabbatical to Spain. It was to be the first time that my family would meet Charles. I was excited and looked forward to the day ahead.

The sun was shining. The sky was clear. The celebration was to be held outside in my mother's garden. We gathered together and everyone was introduced to each other, Charles engaged the crowd in his usual, larger than life style. The day went well. I was pleased.

Later that afternoon, I needed to lie down. I was experiencing stomach and back pains. Charles was not overly attentive to me. He seemed far more occupied with making an impression on my family. My mother brought me a cup of tea and enquired as to how I was feeling. I was having increasing pains around my abdominal area. They were pains like small contractions. I decided to tell my mother that I was expecting Charles's child. She was overwhelmed with happiness and joy. I explained that I did not want anyone to know at this time as we were waiting for our forthcoming engagement to happen first.

Charles asked for me and he was directed up to the bedroom. I explained to him about the pains I was having and we decided that it would be appropriate to return home. Charles treated me with kid gloves. He looked after me with tenderness and care that I had not experienced before. It was in the middle of the night when the worst happened. Our baby had decided that she was not going to join us in this world. The pain was intense. It continued for a couple of days. The doctor prescribed an internal check to make sure that everything had left my body and that I was physically healthy.

It was a kind of grief that I had not experienced before. I had travelled, emotionally, from total surprise at the prospect of having a new family member to losing the wonderful gift that had been bestowed upon me.

While I tried to let life take up its more usual level of emotional intensity, the trauma and depth of sadness at the loss of our baby came to rest in a special place inside my heart.

THERAPEUTIC ANALYSIS: LOSING SIGHT OF REALITY

Charles's response to my telephone call was to distance himself. He was abrupt and unresponsive. He may have felt irritated by my neediness, not to mention the intrusion into his other life.

When he reflected on the telephone conversation, he may have felt compelled to resolve the situation in case he had overstepped the mark and prompted me to abandon him and quit the relationship.

The experience of pregnancy shows how far removed from reality and emotional safety I was. My extreme feelings had overwhelmed my instinct to keep my sons and myself safe. I had been lost in immaturity and fantasy to such an extent that I had been willing to bring another child into the world, the consequences of which would have been far reaching.

I had abandoned my self-care through the depth and haze of the Love Addict fantasy and as a result I had not taken sufficient birth control precautions. After the miscarriage, I moved back, rapidly, into the denial and fantasy of the relationship, continuing the Love Addiction.

Operating in extremes is another significant sign of Love Addiction in action. Most addicts will not be interested in moderation and therefore will be drawn towards black or white thinking or distorted thinking in the extremes; the middle ground seems boring. (This is described in more detail in Chapter 12: Achieving balance within your relationship.*)*

November

After the half term break from school, when the children had spent their holiday with their friends at their friends' family home, the school loosened its grip on visiting and contact with the boys. I was relieved. Patrick and Joseph came home and we began to heal the trauma and pain that had been inflicted.

I had been waiting now, for some time, to meet the friends and family Charles talked about so often. It seemed only natural that I should be introduced to them. Charles was always just putting the phone down from his family as I entered the room. Opportunities seemed to escape me all the time. Charles assured me that his family was very excited to meet me and our engagement was the best time for that to happen.

The first introduction came by way of a dinner with a dear friend of Charles that he had known for about eleven years, Lord Julian Winterbottom and his partner Sarah.

We were to meet them in London at Julian's home. Charles decided that it was best for us to stay the night in London. His home was unusable because of the construction work, so he chose a hotel close by.

The hotel was small and certainly not five star, but Charles was always unusual, if not a little eccentric in his behaviour so I did not place a great deal of importance on this. Besides, his eccentricity was one of his endearing characteristics.

We settled into the hotel and began to get ready for the evening. Charles put his hand on my face and told me how much he loved me. He claimed to be the happiest man on earth. We made sweet love and proceeded to meet up with his friends.

This was my first opportunity to get to know the people Charles had so proudly and lovingly talked about. We exchanged pleasantries over cocktails in Julian's home. They seemed a delightful couple. Charles had told me before that he really did not care for Sarah. He thought she was a dangerous woman, and he told me some of the manipulative things she had done. I decided to take her as I found her. I found nothing to worry me at first.

We proceeded to the restaurant. We placed our orders and then the conversations began. Charles and Julian became entrenched quite quickly and Sarah took the opportunity to engage me in conversation. It was not long before she asked me about Charles's girlfriend. I was surprised that she would ask me a question like this, as it was quite obvious that I was Charles's girlfriend. I began to feel confused. I noticed feeling physically uncomfortable. I replied that I was Charles's girlfriend and did not know what she meant. Sarah insisted that Charles had another girlfriend. Her name was Catherine.

'Oh, Catherine,' I exclaimed. I felt a great sense of relief.

'Catherine is Charles's pupil barrister in his Chambers,' I replied.

Sarah still insisted that Catherine was Charles's girlfriend. My body became hot and my vision and hearing became impaired. What was this woman saying to me? Surely she could see that Charles and I were totally in love and together. We were practically living together. How could Charles have another girlfriend? He had told me that he had not had another love relationship since his first marriage ended twenty years before.

My body and mind felt as though they were about to explode. I noticed that Charles was watching me. I seized the opportunity so quickly that any thoughts about holding back did not have a chance to stop me.

'Charles, I have a question.' I said this in quite a loud voice, so as to hold his attention. 'This may make you feel uncomfortable, and I apologise for that, but is Catherine your girlfriend?'

Charles's face was shocked and frozen in disbelief. 'I refuse to answer that question,' he replied.

'You just did,' I answered.

With that, I excused myself and went to the ladies' room, my heart pounding and my shock taking hold. He had been lying to me.

I returned to the table and we all made small talk that felt decidedly uncomfortable. Mercifully, time passed swiftly and we said our goodbyes.

Charles hailed a cab and we left for the hotel. Charles began to explode in the cab. I noticed the driver look at me in the rear view mirror with concern. I was clear that I did not want to talk about the situation at that time as it was too late in the evening and I wanted to leave it for the morning.

I did not sleep, for the thoughts of Charles lying to me were too disturbing. Charles reached out to me at about five in the morning. I shunned him.

'You lied to me,' I said.

Charles flew into another tirade of abuse.

I got up, collected my things and left. I felt deserted and distraught, numb and confused.

That day I heard nothing from him. I turned my attention to work and buckled down to finishing my course assignments, a way of diverting my obsessive thoughts and denying the pain of what was happening. I guess I did not want to confront the dreadful truth that Charles had been lying to me. If he lied about this what else had he told me lies about? It was a chilling question to contemplate. I went to sleep that night with heaviness in my heart and emptiness in my soul.

The following morning the telephone rang. It was Charles.

'I have missed you. I love you,' he said with a weak soft voice, like a destroyed man hoping for forgiveness.

'I have missed you, too,' I said.

'I'll be there in an hour,' was his response.

Down went the receiver and an hour later Charles was standing at the door. He looked tired and dishevelled. He showered and dressed for the day ahead. A lunch appointment was in the diary for Thursday and neither one of us wanted to cancel it. We wanted life to continue on the happy note it had sounded for the previous five months.

Lunch was pleasant. We spent it in good company with a dear friend and colleague of mine. On our return to my apartment, the subject of the previous few days did not arise. We were skilful in our avoidance at that time, perhaps knowing that it would be raised sometime later, when the dust had settled.

THERAPEUTIC ANALYSIS: A DEFINING MOMENT

Learning that Charles had a girlfriend signified the moment when denial in our relationship was finally shattered. Together with losing the protection afforded by denial came shock. The fantasy relationship no longer retained its power and strength. Feelings such as rage, revenge and depression are likely to follow this stage of the Love Addiction cycle. This is the time when the Love Addict may choose either to leave the relationship or to re-enter it in the hope that she can hold on to her original fantasy. So powerful is the fantasy that it can destroy lives and it often does.

I chose to re-enter the relationship, although I had evidence of betrayal from the dinner with Charles's friends in London. The evidence was hurtful, but it also gave me an element of power in the relationship. I could use that information as revenge against Charles if I needed to hold him hostage in the future. The Love Addict may take revenge, using information, as an expression of the pain of withdrawal from the fantasy. This pain may also show itself as rage, shame, depression or panic.

We need to examine the rewards for staying in such a relationship both for the Love Addict and for the Love Avoidant. The Love Addict is desperate for the fantasy to be real. The Love Avoidant has much the same fantasy, only underpinned with different anxieties. (A further explanation of the aspects of this personality type is given in Chapter 13: The love avoidant personality.)

December

The following day a call came about my youngest son, who wanted to come home, as he was feeling ill. Charles and I collected him on the Friday morning and brought him home. The following day was the parent-teachers' meeting at the school, at which we would review Joseph's work and progress.

We talked with Joseph's teachers and received their feedback on his progress and potential. Once the meeting was over, we decided to skip the school lunch, which was provided on such occasions, and go home.

As we got in the car Charles complained about feeling ill. He thought he might have a touch of the 'flu. I held my hand to his head but could feel no signs of fever. On our return to the apartment Charles wanted to lie down. I went about taking care of Joseph, while also keeping an eye on Charles. I had taken on a nurturing role, a role that I enjoyed for now I could give Charles back some of the caring that had previously been so generously given to me in my times of need.

Charles's feeling ill did not provide the opportunity for us to confront the real issues that we so desperately needed to address. I guess a part of me was also grateful for this opportunity to procrastinate. It kept the inevitable from happening. My mind was numbing out to the enormity of the situation. Charles would have to have a very convincing story to tell.

Meanwhile, Joseph continued to play Monopoly in the sitting room, keeping quiet and taking the time to heal in peace and in the comfort of his own home.

My real concerns were with Charles, as he still claimed to feel unwell. He certainly looked pale and more worrying than anything was the fact that he was not complaining. He was quiet. Past experience told me that silence in illness was a sign of genuine ill health. Charles was not complaining. Perhaps it was just another way in which he showed to me that he was different to other men?

Charles refused to eat that night, although he did join Joseph in a game of Monopoly. He became animated and the friendly arguing that went on led me to think that Charles was not as ill as I had thought. I enjoyed watching my son and Charles playing together. I had hope in my heart that things would be sorted between us. Surely Charles could not have lied to me.

With both Joseph and Charles tucked up in bed, I decided to retire to bed, too, and rest from my inner whirlpool of doubts and reassurances.

The following morning started with a blaze of sunlight, a beautiful day. It was early December and there was crispness in the air. I was so looking forward to Christmas, the end of what had been an enormously stressful year.

I held the hope that a potentially happy, loving relationship would flourish. I had managed to minimise the seriousness of what had happened that night in London with Charles's friends. The truth got in the way of my fantasy and my fantasy was my lifeline. It helped me to survive and distract me from the trauma of what was happening in the other areas of my life, especially the legal battle, not only with respect to finances but also to my concerns with Patrick and Joseph's safety and security.

Charles spent the day in bed, not even getting up for Sunday lunch.

Joseph and I passed a relaxing day together and, eventually, the time came for him to return to school. I remember it clearly. Charles jumped out of bed and insisted on taking the journey back to school with Joseph and me. The night was black and the rain had decided to pour down. It was bleak. I tried to refuse to let Charles make the long journey, but he was most insistent and, as usual, his authoritative manner won.

We arrived at the school, left the car to look for Patrick and say our hellos to him. We found him in the dormitory and embraced. Joseph and I hugged each other and we arranged to talk the following day.

The return car journey seemed long. The silence was palpable. It was the first time that Charles and I had been on our own. 'We don't need to get engaged so soon now. I think we should wait,' Charles ventured.

My mind was racing as we sat at the traffic lights waiting for the green light to move on.

'Well, that concerns me,' I said with a hint of aggression.

'What do you mean?' fired back Charles.

'Well, you wanted to marry me. You took it as your right. You were not prepared to wait. Yet you have made no attempt to buy the engagement ring that you have promised me many times to secure our commitment to each other and, now, you say that you think we should wait!'

I was sure things were not right now. He was not proving to be the man of honour he had so many times assured me he was.

Charles quietened down. He could see that I was in a fighting mood and he probably did not have strength to defend himself and fight back. We completed the rest of the journey in silence. Charles put himself to bed immediately. I got into bed with him and switched on the television. The volume was low, so as not to disturb him. Soon, he was asleep.

I turned out the light and hoped for the bliss of sleep. All through the night Charles was up and down visiting the bathroom. On one occasion I remember him running a bath. He said it would soothe him. I felt exhausted with all the disturbances through the night, but tried not to show it.

Early that morning, I took Charles to the doctor to check out what was happening to him.

The doctor assured him that he had gastroenteritis and advised him to return to bed and he gave me a list of foods and drinks that would be helpful. Charles returned home and I went into the town to do the shopping. I went to the bank to check up on the transfer of funds from the sale of my summer home in Spain – I seemed to be waiting for hours. Charles had encouraged the sale of my Spanish house on the grounds that he already owned a villa in Spain and we did not need another. Spain was my heaven – I simply loved being there.

Caught in my thoughts, I became depressed and soulful. Thoughts were surfacing now about Charles – his lies – and the fact that I had sold my place in Heaven while relying on his version of truth. As much as my psyche wanted to believe that this man was my knight in shining armour, my intellect would not let me practise the self-deceit any longer. My body became tight and uncomfortable with the realisation.

I left the bank without the information and returned home.

Charles was sitting in a chair. I took my place opposite him. My tears began to fall, quite involuntarily. Charles could see the distress clearly in my whole being.

'What is it, Alice?' he said in a sad voice.

'Charles, I have shown you nothing but kindness, trust and honesty, I have been loyal and have stood by you as you have been kind to me, but I can't ignore what is happening. You have clearly lied to me and now I can't help thinking that I don't know what else you have lied about.'

My tears fell without a sound. They simply streamed down my face as I sat before the man I loved so deeply and dearly, knowing that this would have to end.

Charles took my hand and led me to the bedroom. He laid me down and placed himself next to me. He asked me to lie there and allow him to lie next to me. He wanted to comfort me without words. Words would not change the truth and he knew it.

Charles seemed to return to his illness. At the point of lying down on the bed, he was uncomfortable. Night fell soon after and another round of restlessness and discomfort took place for him. I had told him that I would sleep in the spare room and let him rest without worrying about disturbing me. At one point, at about five in the morning I got up to see how he was as I could hear that he was disturbed. He told me that he would be travelling to London that morning as he had an appointment with the Belgian Ambassador. He also wanted to take a gift for the girls in the office at the Embassy.

I told him he was not being sensible about travelling and that he should reconsider.

Charles returned to bed.

At seven o'clock in the morning he told me that he was in severe pain and wanted to see a doctor soon.

I called the doctors' surgery, but no one was there. It was too early. He needed to wait half an hour for the surgery to open. He was clearly in pain and was finding it difficult to find comfort in any position. Finally, the surgery opened and the doctor suggested we come in immediately. We arrived and the doctor examined and questioned Charles. Charles's answers seemed to shock the doctor. The doctor's instructions were to wait in the waiting room while he made a telephone call to the hospital. Charles struggled to the waiting room and it was no time before he collapsed. The doctor came to see him and told me to take him immediately to the hospital. It would be quicker than waiting for an ambulance. We managed to get Charles into the car and I sped off.

On arrival, it seemed a long time before Charles was admitted. The message from the doctors' surgery, informing them of his arrival, didn't appear to have got through, which slowed things down. Eventually, Charles was lifted on to a bed and now tests were carried out. The pain he was in was clear. Nothing seemed to help. The doctor had inserted an intravenous drip of morphine to help him with the pain but even this was no relief. Eventually, they increased the amount of morphine.

I asked Charles if I should call Andrea, his personal assistant, but Charles did not want to disturb anybody. He did not want them alarmed. I was concerned that a man of his standing should be in a National Health hospital in Surrey without any of his staff or family knowing or having the opportunity to transfer him to a private hospital. I broached this several times when Charles seemed a little stronger, but he was adamant that nobody should know his whereabouts.

The space was limited in the tiny cubicle that separated each patient. I leaned close to Charles and told him that when he was better we would go to a health spa and get strong and fit. He agreed and smiled at me.

They took Charles off for an X-ray and I waited for his return. His face was ashen. He was in great pain. The movement from the bed to have the X-ray had been too much. More doctors came to visit and check up on him. Blood tests were taken and his blood pressure was checked time after time. Eventually, they moved Charles into a ward. He seemed calmer.

My mobile phone rang. It was the school. Joseph was in trouble; he had upset another pupil and the school was asking me to collect him for a time of reflection. I explained that it was difficult as I was in the hospital, but they were insistent and seemed not to care about my personal situation. I left Charles at six that evening. He was calm and assured me he would be fine while I attended to Joseph.

On arrival at the school, Joseph was waiting for me and began to explain his innocence.

I had expected psychological reactions from both Patrick and Joseph after the shock and trauma they had both experienced as a result of me challenging their father. Joseph and I arrived home and I prepared dinner. I was exhausted. I had not had so much as a cup of tea to drink or anything to eat all day. I called Charles later to check that he was all right. He told me that he had spoken to Andrea and that she was handling things for him and that she would inform his family. I was relieved.

I prepared my clothes for a quick departure that night, just in case I had an urgent phone call. Something didn't feel right.

Early in the morning, I left the apartment to see Charles. I had left food for Joseph and told him that if he needed anything to call me. He was set up for a hard day's study at home.

I arrived at the hospital ward, to find Charles had been moved to another ward. The lady in the ward Charles had been in when I left him told me that he had had a terrible night. Not long after I found Charles. He looked ashen and afraid. He asked me to shave him and I did. It was not an easy task, as he now seemed so fragile. He told me he was feeling fine, but his appearance belied his words. Two nursing assistants arrived to change the bed. They moved Charles into the chair beside the bed. Within a minute Charles slumped as the colour drained from his face. They rushed into action and placed the oxygen mask over his face. The doctor on duty arrived and they did what was needed to bring him back to consciousness. Things were clearly not going well and I wanted some answers. What were they doing to help him?

I left to speak with the sister in charge of his ward. She could simply give me no information. They did not know what was wrong with him. That day saw test after test, doctor after doctor.

At midday I called my mother to explain the situation. As I spoke to her, my tears began to fall. I knew something was terribly wrong with Charles. With some determination, I composed myself, as I knew that once I lost control of my fear I would be incapable of helping him.

It was an impossible situation. Despite all my misgivings, I called the school to speak with the Headmaster and ask if Joseph could return. The situation at the hospital was so desperate I could not leave. His phone went to answer phone and I left a message for him to call me. He did not. At three o'clock, with Joseph's permission, I very reluctantly called Joseph's father and asked him to go to the apartment and collect Joseph, as I knew I could not look after him properly, given the situation. He did so and so I had one less immediate worry. I tried not to think about what he might be saying to Joseph.

I went back to see Charles. As I approached him after this short absence, the illness was clear to see. He had become much worse. I held his hand and assured him that everything would be all right; I wouldn't leave him. Again, I asked him if I could have the number to call Andrea or perhaps his son. Charles would have none of it. Charles was a formidable character, not someone to challenge, and certainly not now that he was so weak.

The doctor came to the bed. They wanted to do a scan. Charles needed to go downstairs to the scanner. I accompanied him, holding his hand all the way, as the bed was wheeled away. We arrived and waited in the public waiting area. People were milling around and Charles had about four student doctors around his bed. It was warm inside the hospital. I made reference to this to one of the doctors just as Charles projectile vomited blood everywhere. It was in his eyes, his hair and all about his bed. I rushed forward to comfort him as the doctors stepped back. Charles's face was afraid and shocked. It took on the look of a child, innocent and helpless. I also knew Charles well enough to know that he would be feeling devastatingly embarrassed that such a thing happening in a public place. Soon after, the auxiliary nurses came to take him away and clean him. The horror was sinking in deeper and deeper as the hours passed by.

Something was seriously wrong with Charles and the doctors did not know what it was.

Charles was wheeled back up to a new ward, a Step Down Unit. This was a small ward with two nurses covering four patients. The aim was to give more care than the usual ward but not so much as intensive care. The doctors crowded around Charles's bed and it was clear that they were at a loss. I could overhear their conversation; it told me what I already knew. Nothing was obvious about Charles's illness. The not knowing was deeply worrying. A surgeon arrived and talked about surgery. Charles looked even more frightened than before. Another doctor had instructed a drain of excess blood from Charles's stomach. An amazing two litres of blood, which had a distinct smell, was drawn off. A new nurse who had just started on the Step Down Unit that day said that she had never seen anything like it before. I was not encouraged by this and wished she had kept her thoughts to herself. The scan showed nothing and the next step was for the doctors to do an endoscopy to see if there were signs of ulceration. If there were no success with that, the next step would be to conduct an exploratory operation. The doctors needed Charles's permission to take him straight from the endoscopy to the operating theatre, but Charles was having none of it. He insisted that first they let him come round fully from the sedation and then tell him of their findings. Only then would he give permission for surgery.

I waited anxiously outside the ward to hear the results. Eventually, they came back and told of their disappointment; nothing could be found through the endoscope. Time needed to pass to allow Charles's blood pressure to resume normality and then for him to be prepared for surgery. The anaesthetist was a German lady, large and forbidding. She checked and re-checked Charles's blood several times. Then the time for surgery arrived and Charles was wheeled down to the lift. I held his hand, kissed him on the head and told him I would be waiting outside for him to return.

I drifted around the hospital not knowing where to put myself and not knowing how long Charles would be. Eventually, I came upon the sister in charge of Charles's ward. She told me that I might as well use the time to go home, freshen up and have something to eat.

I took her advice. I was shattered. On my arrival home I noticed that many messages had been left on my answerphone. I did not have the time to listen to them, and I began to prepare something to eat. The telephone rang and I picked up the receiver.

'Hello, is that Mrs Bertrand?' The voice from the other end said.

'It's Charles Bertrand's partner. Who is it please?' I replied.

'This is the hospital. There is something that we need your advice on. Can you come back and make your way to the operating theatre?' asked the man.

'Of course. I'll come immediately.' I replaced the receiver.

I was surprised at the speed with which I was recalled to the hospital and wondered why they wanted my advice. I left my apartment and sped back to the hospital.

Eventually, I found the operating theatre. A young doctor whom I recognised from earlier in the day appeared. 'Follow me, please. I'll take you through to the office.' He seemed tense.

I followed him through and took a seat as requested. I waited for the surgeon to arrive. She came through the door and calmly told me that she had important news for me.

'Charles is dying. We have tried everything possible. He has a strangulated bowel and there is nothing we can do to help him.'

My mind went numb and my body froze. I did not know what to do next.

'Can't you attach a colostomy bag?' I asked in desperation.

'There is nothing to attach anything to. The bowel is completely strangulated. There must have been a clot in his blood that blocked the blood supply to the bowel. If only Charles had complained more about the pain. We would have expected more reaction from him in this condition. He was very brave,' she said.

My thoughts ran wild. Why didn't he complain more? What would I do next?

The surgeon asked me if I would like to see him in the operating theatre to be with him as he came round from the anaesthetic. I said yes, and asked what I should say to him if he were to ask how things went. She told me that I could tell him he was very poorly. I thought this was a kind thing to say. My heart was full of dread and pain. I entered the theatre and went over to Charles. He began to come around. He opened his eyes and I smiled at him.

'Hello, darling,' I said.

Charles was groggy and didn't reply. I held his hand and followed the bed down to a private room. He was linked up to various machines that checked his heart rate and blood pressure, and to a morphine drip.

I sat in the chair beside him, tired and in shock, mustering up all the strength I had to reassure him that things would be all right but without telling him the hard facts.

Eventually, he muttered, 'How did it go?'

'Darling, you are very poorly. Relax. I am here by your side. I won't leave you,' I said, hoping that my sadness and shock would not show through.

'Was it a success?' he asked 'Any more operations?'

I told him that he did not need any more operations and that things were going as well as could be expected, that he was very poorly and that it was necessary to inform Andrea and his family so that they could visit him and support him. Charles was adamant, even in this state, that he did not want to inform anyone.

I felt frustrated about this but I was powerless, as I had no way of contacting them myself. I sat there by his side watching him slip in and out of a peaceful sleep. Occasionally, Charles would ask for some water, which he would call champagne. The nurses tried to limit his intake of fluid so I was in a battle between Charles and the nurses. Charles easily won the battle; his dying wishes were, of course, my command.

Sometimes Charles would perk up and say, 'I'm so happy'. The smile on his face was that of a little child, the look in his eyes resembled that first glance that sealed our love on that day back in July. Just six months earlier.

I wondered at his comment. Did he know he was dying? Was he trying to keep me happy by saying this? I was confused.

The room was dark and very warm; my chair was becoming more and more uncomfortable as I had been sitting in it for so long. Occasionally, I would sit on Charles's bed to be closer to him.

I was weary and shocked. How long would this last? I longed to let go of my pain and cry my heart dry. But I could not let Charles see my distress; I had to be strong for him. I can remember thinking, please let him slip away now. I didn't think I had any more strength to go on, but I did. Charles passed away, peacefully without pain at 2.55 a.m. on a cold December morning.

I held him in my arms and cried while I said goodbye to my darling. The priest arrived to serve his blessings on Charles's spirit. I was ushered out of the room to allow the nurses to do their job. They tidied him up and I was allowed to visit his body. I sat looking at him, so peaceful and content.

A taxi took me back to my apartment where I let out my pain and suffering of the last forty-eight hours. I poured myself a brandy, which I could not drink. I lay down to rest, but could not. As seven o'clock arrived I began to think of all the practical things that needed to be done. I didn't want to be the only one to know Charles's fate. His family needed to know.

That same day I called the Embassy.

THERAPEUTIC ANALYSIS: SHOCK, DISBELIEF, PAIN AND SHAME
Denial and fantasy had taken their hold on me and again I had re-entered the fantasy relationship. The sudden death of Charles was traumatic in itself and, because of my Love Addiction, I now had to come to terms with the many lies that he had told me. He had created for me a completely and utterly false existence.

I felt shock, disbelief, pain and shame. Anger came later, for anger was not an emotion that I knew easily how to express and some months passed before I could feel an appropriate level of anger towards Charles.

Denial in the face of what is painfully obvious to those outside the relationship is common in Love Addiction. When denial is broken, because something the partner does or says is so abusive or so shocking, it may be overlooked should the Love Addict choose to re-enter the relationship. This behaviour perpetuates a swing from a glorious intensity to a baffling distance or withdrawal. The volatility of the relationship and its exquisite intensity can become addictive, as body and brain start to depend on the rushes of adrenaline. Living on the edge makes the Love Addict feel truly alive. Of course, in time each partner starts to realise that they cannot live at such a pace: each one will need to spend long periods of time alone – or seek distraction – in order to recover from such intense stress.

The anxiety of no longer feeling loved, or connected, leads to the desperate need for the familiar intensity when the Love Addict finds herself in the withdrawal stage of the relationship. Reconnection with the relationship helps soothe the anxiety state, which is a biological response to the trauma of no longer feeling loved or valued. Other behaviours may feature in the relationship as a way of maintaining the connection. Sex, for example, is often used as a way of keeping the partner hooked in the relationship; sex also can act as a conduit for the Love Addict to feel loved and valued. Crossover addictions, in which an established addiction transforms itself into another compulsive or addictive behaviour, are common: they reflect the need to be soothed emotionally and represent a form of self-medication.

Paradoxically, the Love Avoidant may conclude that the Love Addict is not so needy, as she appears to cope well on her own. He may be tricked into thinking that he will not be taken over by her neediness. This is likely to relieve his fears and, when he feels relaxed again, he reconnects to his subconscious pattern of relating and begins to take care. She then returns to her subconscious fantasy pattern and once again becomes the needy child. The Love Addict tends to feel that she has a diminished identity if she is not in a relationship. Paradoxically, again, the Love Addict is highly capable of coping alone, out of a relationship.

Because the Love Avoidant is excessively caring, attempting to soothe the Love Addict, in what the Love Avoidant may interpret as his role, there is a struggle for identity between the two addicts. During the struggle, which will feel like paradise to the Love Addict, she will give up her sense of self and effectively abandon herself and her world, friends and family included, in order to retain her partner as her knight in shining armour, effectively her higher power. The Love Addict is attracted by the willingness of the Love Avoidant to take care of her, even though she is very capable of coping alone. This impossible, and dysfunctional, situation traps both people in the love relationship as they attempt, in vain, to resolve childhood abandonment (the emotional or physical absence of a primary caregiver, normally the parent) or enmeshment (an overly close and unbalanced caring relationship between child and primary carer).

Chapter
2

Reflection......and reality

The following weeks took me on a journey of discovery. I felt like a detective. I searched through all of Charles's belongings and found his diary and address book. I went through the entries in it one by one, searching for the truth of what and with whom I had just had this most brief and intense relationship. Fantasy and obsession had hidden the truth.

Reality glimpsed

As reality slowly began to dawn and my world fragmented, I began to doubt who 'I' was. My fantasy had taken such a strong hold over me that when reality entered my consciousness it was absolutely overwhelming.

My detective work led me to Catherine, Charles's pupil barrister ......or girlfriend. I called her to inform her of Charles's death and discovered that we had much more in common than I had first guessed. We arranged to meet at Victoria Station. It turned out Catherine was, indeed, a barrister. We embraced like two old friends. It was ironic; we had both loved the man who had deceived us both and now we were brought together through his death. Affectionately, over cups of coffee, we planned his funeral, which was finally organised with the kind help of my friend, Father Godfrey, a priest.

We laid three roses on Charles's coffin and bade him farewell.

I believe that Charles needed his elaborate fantasy world, as his own reality was too painful for him. As Catherine and I picked our way through the stories that Charles had told, we tried to put together the reality and the psychology of the man we knew as Charles.

The search for truth

I had made contact with the Belgian Embassy and they in turn made contact with Charles's family. He did indeed have three children but his daughter was not a coroner. None of the children wished to attend their father's funeral. Their only concern was if Charles had left any estate.

The grand mansion that Charles had told me was his and was being renovated did not belong to him. It was Catherine who owned the basement flat and the rest of the mansion was divided into individual residential and commercial apartments. In truth, it seemed that Charles did not possess anything of financial significance. No Spanish villa, no Rolls Royce, no country house in Cornwall. He had concocted stories with such detail and told his lies with such utter conviction that now it sent a chill down my spine. He was very detailed about the banking business that he told me he was involved in; Catherine and I explored Charles's stories and tried to make sense of them.

The picture of Charles's life now began to take quite a different shape to the one he had portrayed. Anger was beginning to stir inside me but I was not able to express it. For years I had learned that naked anger was unacceptable; now, I was struggling with the inner conflict between needing to explode with anger and to suppress it.

Catherine thought that Charles was involved with a money-laundering outfit. She had often seen Charles sewing the inside of his jacket and travelling back and forward from South Africa. This may have explained why he knew so much about money and banking.

We wondered if Charles had spent time in prison in Spain as he had a good knowledge of Spanish law, spoke fluent Spanish and seemed to know a lot about the politics of the country. While the scars on Charles's head and leg were clearly real, neither Catherine nor I could accept his claim that they were bullet wounds. That said, however, what we pieced together does add up to a rather sinister past.

I was becoming increasingly astounded at my inability to have seen through his elaborate lies and deceit. My feelings of shame resonated, physically, through my body.

Catherine was a joint signatory to a bank account that Charles used. She was able to access the account to establish what funds he had. Ironically, Charles had almost exactly the correct amount to pay for his own funeral. Catherine withdrew the funds and gave them to me to pay the undertaker.

Catherine and I had become quite close in a strange sort of way. I found myself doing detective work with a woman that I did not know, trying to establish the elements of truth about the man with whom we had both shared our lives. We were both very curious to find out more about Charles's activities. We found a set of keys in Charles's belongings: Catherine could identify some of them and I could identify mine. However, there was one key that was different. It looked like the key of a safety deposit box. Catherine and I looked at each other and agreed that we needed to investigate further. We tried to think of the likely, and con-venient, places that Charles might have had a safety deposit box.

We both embraced our new roles of playing detective. We tried the safety deposit boxes at Victoria Rail Station, Waterloo Rail Station and King's Cross Rail Station. We tried other well-known sites for safety deposit boxes. Alas, Catherine and I had, eventually, to accept that noth-ing was to be found.

Quite what we thought we would find is beyond me; on reflection, I think the most important part of our search was a process of trying to make sense of the situation.

Other women

From the spring following his death, I continued my search mostly alone and, from Charles's address book, I made contact with an old friend of his in Belgium. He told me that Charles had left Belgium because of a big scandal involving his family's printing business; again, thoughts ran to money laundering and fraud. Charles's friend asked if I had made contact with another of his friends in Belgium. A woman. He gave me her number.

I was hesitant about having this number. Apprehensively, I called. The lady informed me that she and Charles were to have been together early in December, the week that Charles died. Though I had feared I would discover something like this, I was still appalled and shocked. I wondered how much more lay in store for me.

After months of reflection, I guess Charles's plan was to leave England as he probably thought I would end the relationship. He had her as his 'stash'. This term is used when an addict collects a safety or fall-back pool of whatever his preferred addiction is; in Charles's case, women. It is not uncommon for Love Addicts and Love Avoidants to have a supply of people, on hold, who can be brought in to the picture to calm and soothe the anxiety of being abandoned by another.

As for Andrea, I found that she did not exist, but I think that she represented that part of Charles's character that helped him to manage his life. She was the imaginary aspect of him that would sort everything out, in effect, a psychological coping device: his own fantasy saviour. This way of coping may also indicate a traumatic event in earlier life that led him to split, or develop another dimension, in order to survive the depth of trauma. (See surviving trauma in Chapter 5: *The burden of shame.*)

Survival mechanism

We can see that Charles used his bogus business dealings to protect himself from intimacy and to manipulate our relationship to his best advantage, while keeping his 'stash' for security. This characterises the Love Avoidant's style of emotional survival and typifies the behaviours that the Love Avoidant may adopt in order to distance himself. This gives him a sense of autonomy and relief from the overwhelming closeness of the relationship that would otherwise make him fear suffocation.

When a person experiences overwhelming feelings of suffocation or of being too close in a relationship, this typically relates to early childhood experiences of being unable to cope with excessive adult demands, typically from the major caregiver (usually a parent). For the Love Avoidant the anxiety of not being able to cope is likely to lead to the person feeling as though life is being drained from him or her and pressure builds due to the demands from the other person's dependency. At this point, even an apparently insignificant trigger, because of the emotional build-up, may lead to an explosion of anger or rage.

Transcending the truth

I had ignored what must have seemed stunningly obvious to others. The Love Addict's fantasy holds her partner as her higher power, believing that she will be rescued and life will be the way she always dreamed it would be. She, the Love Addict, will be taken care of. This way of interpreting a relationship is medication for the Love Addict trying to survive the traumatic, emotional pain – the pain of feeling unlovable – that set her on the path of Love Addiction in the first place.

This emotional pain may have resulted from abandonment or rejection or some other emotional deprivation experienced in early life. In my case, I had made the love relationship with Charles a priority above all else and in doing so had put at risk the true, valuable relationships I had with my friends and family. They had wondered so often at the genuineness of Charles, gently trying to speak to me about him, without wanting to destroy my world, which they could so clearly see was now built upon him.

Obsession in a relationship is likely to distance the obsessed partner from other life relationships that need attending to. Neglect can easily happen within a family system. The vulnerability of the Love Addict in this fog of relating may lead her to be overly willing to permit her partner to take major decisions in her life, as in my experience with regard to legal affairs. Thinking about the implications still chills me. We can also see how important it is that denial is successfully broken so that the Love Addict can step back from the situation and contemplate reality.

I had chosen to deny any of the obvious truths about Charles and the reality of our relationship until the night of the dinner in London. The first introduction to Charles's friends was the evening that my deep state of denial was painfully breached. I responded immediately by having an anxiety attack at the table. Breaking denial is a very anxious time for a Love Addict. My extreme level of anxiety manifested itself as a temporary loss of both vision and hearing.

Punishing the Love Avoidant partner

I was still barely able to speak but I mustered the energy to confront Charles at the table in front of his friends. My withdrawal from the relationship came some hours later during the night, as I again confronted his lies and witnessed his defensive aggression when he tried to conceal his blatant untruths.

Withdrawal is the stage, within the illness of Love Addiction, that follows denial and can lead to intense feelings of rage, depression, panic or shame. This was when I left Charles, only to be reeled back into the relationship by the sound of his voice and his desperate plea for 'love' two days later.

I was quick to resume the fantasy, still desperate for my knight in shining armour. Surely he did exist? Charles's illness and death brought a conclusion earlier than would otherwise have been the case, but the relationship was more than likely to have been doomed to seesaw, from intensity to withdrawal, and to be volatile, until I could no longer deny reality. Such seesawing is a desperate attempt to reconnect to the initial intensity of the relationship. It represents the broken love cycle from the Love

Addict's earliest love experience, her original love relationship with the parental figure.

It is usual for the seesaw to continue until exhaustion and disillusionment take over, for denial to be broken and truth finally to be victorious. The desperate attempts by the Love Addict to receive love create a neediness that is often overwhelming for the love partner. While the neediness is exhausting for both the Love Addict and the love partner, the driving intensity of obsession and compulsion provide the fuel.

Disillusionment becomes unavoidable

The Love Addict, when in a relationship, is so desperate to have her fix of love she may seem insatiable and may appear never to have enough love shown to her. Her physical health may be damaged as a result of the self-defeating neediness of Love Addiction. The psychological torture that I experienced through Charles's life and death led to the start of a stomach ulcer and digestive problems. My physical health suffered badly as a result of my catastrophic love-addicted relationship. The stress and anxiety caused by pathological grief led to the collapse of my immune system. I spent several months healing before travelling to Arizona to continue my counselling career.

It was at the beginning of the following year that I realized how ill I had been at the end of my stay in Arizona. I had contracted Valley Fever, a fungal infection that is ingested into the lungs. It is particularly apparent during the rainy seasons in Arizona.

Unfortunately, my immune system has still not fully recovered and I remain susceptible to a relapse at any time. This can be a serious life long problem.

Love Addiction is a serious psychological illness with potentially devastating consequences. People may ask why I have chosen to divulge such personal and detailed information about my own experience. My view is that it may help to show just how serious the condition is. Professional integrity has supported my decision to make this personal disclosure, despite the risk of judgment by others. Having shared my story with colleagues, I have been encouraged to disclose the severity of the illness, together with the distress and shame associated with it.

Where was my inner voice?

Many people have asked me why I did not check out what Charles told me. Whatever happened to my gut instinct?

- ❤ Why was I not more cautious around this man and more questioning of his wildly elaborate stories?
- ❤ If only I had checked out his home in Cornwall……
- ❤ Why had I not insisted on meeting some of his family?
- ❤ I could, perhaps, have checked his identity on the Internet instead of believing what I was told
- ❤ I could have insisted on meeting his barrister pupil, Catherine, and his PA Andrea
- ❤ Why didn't I question his lack of letter writing to me when I was in Spain, despite his promise of writing to me every day?

When reality is in balance, this is what we do. However, when functioning in a love-addicted state, the risk of having the fantasy destroyed is too great and, so, denial protects the Love Addict from reality spoiling a comfort zone, which is, in fact, utterly dysfunctional. The denial, furthermore, exposes the Love Addict to substantial psychological risks, from which there can be no protection.

Pathological grief

The profound grief I felt meant that I was terrified that when I went to sleep I would never wake up. I visited the doctor time after time until he told me that I was making myself extremely sick. The shock of those words was enough to make a difference. It was as though another shock were needed to break my own denial. It is not unusual where trauma is apparent in someone's life that a need for trauma may develop; the need is to stay connected, to feel alive. This could be the reason for the success of TV soap dramas. The trauma experience perhaps becomes normalised.

'Pathological grief' is 'The intensification of grief to the level where the person is overwhelmed, resorts to maladaptive behaviour, or remains interminably in the state of grief without progression of the mourning process towards completion. [It] involves processes that do not move progressively towards assimilation or accommodation, but lead to stereotyped repetitions or extensive interruptions of healing.' (Horowitz et al.)

When healing starts

The classic processes of bereavement – denial, anger, grief and acceptance – each overlapping with the other, gradually unfolded. My obsessive fear of death and dying lessened and I began to sleep through the night without having someone else stay in the apartment with me. My digestive system was, however, still disturbed.

I decided to take an extended break to heal my body and soul. I travelled to Spain to recover my health in a calming atmosphere. After a few months, I flew back to London to seek help from a Tibetan doctor who gave me medicine that cured my digestive problems. I did not relapse with pathological grief after this time, for, by now, I had rebuilt my physical and psychological strength and I had acknowledged, and felt, my anger and released it.

During my recovery friends and family had been very supportive. One of my closest friends had asked if I would be interested spending some time in a professional role at The Meadows Treatment Center for Trauma and Addictions in Arizona, USA. My friend was involved in the therapeutic community and was therefore able to arrange for me to go to the centre as a visiting therapist. That autumn I headed for Arizona, my heart weary but my mind open.

I finally touched down at the Meadows and, now hungry for knowledge, devoured all I could. The depth of knowledge I found there was phenomenal. I took in the information quickly and wondered in the presence of such great teachers as Dr Patrick Carnes, who brings so much experience and wisdom to the field. I experienced the magical touch of Pia Mellody. What I gleaned from all this was that many who have never contemplated therapy would benefit from understanding simple behavioural patterns, which can be altered to help healthy functioning and bring about successful relationships.

The processes of recovery

Acceptance and recovery came gradually after my time absorbing the work of Pia Mellody and Dr Patrick Carnes. Their work showed clearly how early in life our bodies and minds can be geared up to suffer Love Addiction, created in the trauma of early childhood experiences. As a result the Love Addict will unwittingly search over and over again for her knight in shining armour.

I realised with a shock that I was a Love Addict.

Commitment to counselling

You will see in this book how the cycle of Love Addiction plays itself out together with the events, traumas and psychological functioning that underpin this addictive behaviour. Chapter 5 *The burden of shame* and Chapter 14 *Taking care of yourself* demonstrate how to restrain the Love Addict from returning to the dysfunctional relationship, showing how you can break free from Love Addiction. Some examples are taken from my private practice, with permission and without identification in order to preserve client confidentiality. I also include personal disclosure to show how trauma and shame from my childhood relate to my own story, described in Chapter 1: *A case of mistaken identity*.

The Love Addict enters a relationship using fantasy, obsession and objectification. That is to say, she creates a false image of her partner. She may take simple information and convert it by using her own interpretation to create an impression of her partner that is quite different from reality. This is to satisfy her need to keep her partner powerful. In doing this, she is distorting reality, becoming mesmerised by addiction to love. At this point the Love Addict is also beginning to abandon herself as she is relinquishing personal power to her partner.

Too little, too much

From one parent, my mother, I received excessive care, attention and love and from the other, my father, rejection and abandonment. The emotional rejection and abandonment that I felt from my father from an early age taught me to try my hardest to gain any affection and reassurance of his love that I could. To me he was my God, he was the father of the family, larger than life and I was desperate for his acceptance. The more I tried, in vain, to gain his attention and love, the more I abandoned myself in the search.

The Love Addict does not have a concept of boundaries (described in Chapter 9) and she will typically suffer from low self-esteem, which is based on shame. She does not know how to use boundaries because she was not taught them. A lack of boundaries can lead to self-destructive behaviours including, for example, 'objectifying' – relating to her partner as an object rather than another human being with vulnerabilities and weaknesses. I did not learn about boundaries from my parents and my father put emotional distance between us, a way of keeping me out of his life in order to protect himself.

My mother encouraged an overly close relationship with me that was inappropriate. It is important that the child is shown emotional maturity by the adult to keep her safe and observe the parent for guidance. Although this overly close relationship may be conducted innocently, without malice, the effect upon the child is that she bears an unreasonable amount of responsibility to maintain her special role: in this way, an enmeshed relationship develops.

Such enmeshment is the style of relationship that creates the Love Avoidant personality. Conversations or information, shared by the adult with the child, which are far too emotionally developed and sophisticated, create a burden for the child. The child needs to grow through appropriate developmental stages in order to live an emotionally balanced life. Around the second year, for example, a child needs to learn that she is no longer the centre of the universe. Her dependency needs for early survival change and the child must now learn that she has limits and boundaries; the word 'NO' is frequently needed to highlight limits and boundaries. It is essential to guide a child through appropriate developmental stages in order to socialise her into society and prepare her for secure relationships. Otherwise, the child may grow up with a feeling of being better than others in the family; indeed, my siblings thought of me as the favourite, although this was not my own perception.

Enmeshed relationships observe few or no boundaries. Consequently, I became my mother's best friend. I was always willing to oblige, which gave me a sense of empowerment and worthiness. The so-called special child creates a separate and confused status for herself in relationships with others. In reality, so-called worthiness is distorted; it is not based on the true worth of the child, but on the worth of the child to the parent. This damages a child's true sense of self; consequently, the child's self-esteem becomes distorted and this is perpetuated in later adult relationships.

While enmeshment may create Love Avoidance, rejection tends to produce a Love Addiction. My mother's influence has produced a tendency in me to be avoidant to women – I quickly fear that they become too needy of me. With men, however, I am more likely to become Love Addicted, fearing their abandonment and trying to change myself in order to conform to their wishes, thus becoming acceptable, and able to feel secure that they will not leave me.

Avoiding intimacy

In my case, I entered the relationship eager to accept Charles's power. I saw him as I wanted to see him, using my fantasy to create who I wanted him to be and not acknowledging who he really was. Significantly, while in my fantasy, I failed to acknowledge the distance that Charles used to avoid intimacy. The message from the Love Avoidant is 'I am all caring', which is tremendously powerful. Because of the pressure of this self-imposed role, the Love Avoidant needs distance in order to find relief and protect himself from becoming drained, or even emotionally suffocated. This thought process reinforces a message to the Love Addict: 'go away but don't leave'.

The Love Addict becomes confused as to why the Avoidant needs to leave her; for desertion represents the ultimate anxiety for her, the threat of abandonment. The message that the Love Addict sends is 'if you leave I will die'. She is desperate to pull in the relationship as close as she can in order to cope with her anxiety. This represents an attempt to heal her wounds from the unmet love needs of childhood. And, yet, paradoxically, distancing in relationships offers a form of comfort to the Love Addict in that it is already familiar through the abandonment she suffered in childhood.

A burning passion

As the addiction progresses, a seesawing – sometimes subtle, sometimes violent – from closeness to distance within the relationship can occur. This creates a profound attachment and, at the same time, confusingly, separation anxiety. The fundamental unconscious aim is to complete the broken cycle of love, which was experienced in childhood but can never be fully resolved: an adult cannot act out as a child, with a child's mind-set of distress, and resolve her unfinished love needs. It is a process that can only be addressed as an adult while nurturing the distress of the inner child. Acknowledging and working with your inner child can be a profound healing experience (see Chapter 5, *The burden of shame.*)

The Love Addict will repeat the cycle in the hope that she will at last receive the care she needed and wanted, together with a loving recognition as a valuable human being, truly worthy of being loved. The need to repeat the cycle, endlessly seeking resolution, creates the compulsion and addiction. The Love Addict becomes hooked on the care and adoration she receives from the partner and the fantasy temporarily obscures her inner need, at times, to be alone. She clings tightly to her denial of emotional abuse by the partner just as firmly as she refutes her partner's distancing mechanisms.

Which pain is preferable?

The Love Addict may decide to isolate herself (imagining isolation to be a relief) from a relationship in order to protect herself from the threat of emotional pain, paradoxically, therefore, embracing the pain of loneliness and loss. Equally, she may opt for the pain of living within a relationship, still experiencing loneliness and loss because of an inability to achieve intimacy.

The Love Addict is likely to invest quite excessive energy into either state, alone or in relationship with another. Either way, emotional pain is the price she pays.

The fire burns out

The Love Addict's inner child is terrified of not being loved and being abandoned. While she enjoys the intensity of the relationship, soothing her anxiety of abandonment, she interprets it as proof that she is valuable and lovable. As we have seen in this chapter, desperate childhood anxiety craves calming. In this way, a powerful connection is created between the Love Addict and the Love Avoidant. The Love Addict, hooked into what she believes to be the truth, experiences the powerful seduction by her love partner as an unrivalled passion. After this initial intensity, the fire may start to burn out and problems will surface, causing a need to revive the initial intensity. Now the Love Addict can choose either to create another type of intensity, by means of an emotional seesaw experience (such as, for example, by creating arguments, by spending too much money, by excessive demands for attention, by drinking to excess), or leave the relationship for another.

I chose more intensity in the relationship with Charles. It is not unusual that, as in any addiction, it can only be satisfied by increasing the dose. Charles's lies and deception were obvious to some people outside our relationship, but it was only at the point of breaching denial, when we had dinner in London with Charles's friends, that I was able to glimpse the truth. This can be viewed as the time when the fire began to burn out. Charles, being the powerful one, enabled me to play the victim and, in turn, use this role to keep him hostage. In other words, I manipulated Charles in order to have my emotional needs met. I was unwilling to let go of my drug of choice, which was Charles.

The Love Addict may now begin to realise that, as she withdraws from the relationship, her Love Avoidant partner will draw closer to her for he may start to suffer his own feelings of abandonment and rejection. He may feel that he is not good enough for her or fear that he is not giving her sufficient care to win her acceptance and approval. Once his feeling of suffocation is reduced, he may feel more able to re-enter the relationship. In this way, with each partner swinging like a pendulum within the relationship, a pattern becomes established, which comprises extreme, intense ways of relating to each other, with heightened break-ups and reconciliations, resulting in emotional exhaustion. And that may become addictive.

The Love Addict may become manipulative, controlling and needy in order to keep her partner close. Denial is broken only when she can face the truth that her partner is emotionally abusing her. (For the purpose of recovery, it may be helpful to view abuse as anything less than nurturing. Abuse can occur through many different behaviours, for example, using distancing as a form of withdrawal from the relationship, excessive work commitments, having casual sexual relationships, alcohol misuse, or any kind of drug use that is inappropriate. (Some people use prescribed drugs of over the counter drugs, so it is not only illegal drugs that may be involved.))

The Love Addict's first glimpse of reality comes with the first chink in her denial. Denial may be used to cope with the original trauma of loss – that is, the loss of love and attention from the primary love relationship, the parent or major caregiver, as you will see as you continue reading this book.

The Love Addict may withdraw from the fantasy relationship as abandonment by the partner becomes clearer. The Love Addict is likely to move into different styles of coping with the pain, such as rage, shame, panic or depression. Each of these emotional states is harmful and, if internalised, can prove self-destructive. A child may find it difficult to express anger and fear, internalising and repressing these emotional feelings in what may be the only way to deal with such emotions at that stage of development.

In severe cases, the Love Addict may exhibit a number of self-destructive behaviours. These include self-harm and self-mutilation, used as a silent expression of repressed feelings and as a means of gaining a sense of control and letting out their pain; eating disorders; obsessive-compulsive behaviours such as pacing up and down; excessive washing and cleaning; rituals such as locking the door several times; and avoiding the cracks in the pavement. These examples and many more behaviours are initiated in order to calm feelings of anxiety and to create a safe living environment. Sadly, these behaviours are often so extreme that they disrupt lives, and, occasionally, may prove fatal with families left devastated. It is my belief that people showing their distress in overt ways such as those listed above are the healthier ones in the family system. It may not at first appear that way because of the extreme methods used to express pain and distress, but they are showing that they need help while other family members may be attempting, successfully, to hide their problems and deny that problems exist.

The typical traits of the Love Addiction cycle include fantasy, denial, panic, withdrawal, distancing, re-engagement, anger, grief, depression and shame. This represents a cycle of emotions and beliefs that is painful and, psychologically, deeply destructive. They can play themselves out in any number of differing styles as there is no set way of going through the cycle.

In the following chapters you will be shown how to take control of Love Addiction and begin a programme of recovery. Anonymous groups such as Love Addiction Anonymous (LAA), Sex & Love Addiction, and Co-Dependence Anonymous (CoDA), and other support groups around the world, can offer additional support to enable you to live your life with healthy self-esteem and relationships that are manageable and joyful to you and to your extended family and friends. A list of international support groups is given at the end of the book.

KEY POINTS

- ♥ Release the trance and open your eyes to reality
- ♥ Break through denial – acknowledge you have a problem
- ♥ Embrace your first step to recovery
- ♥ Seek the support you need.

Chapter
3

The Balance of Emotional Energy

In my relationship with Charles, I gave the maximum amount of energy I could, by fantasising, hour by hour, about the relationship and sometimes by isolating myself in order to maintain my fantasy of Charles. Ultimately, this resulted in the abandonment of my true self.

The needy parent

As I reflect, I can see how the child-parent relationship affects an adult love relationship. In childhood I devoted excessive amounts of energy to my father in order to try to secure the love I wanted but never received. My fate was now determined: I would repeat this pattern in almost every love relationship in my adult life. In return, I expected my partners to dedicate excessive amounts of energy to me, essentially caretaking me. My demands were insatiable and energy draining, creating an emotional neediness within each relationship. Charles and my other partners coped with my neediness by distancing themselves, using work commitments or sex to find relief and escape.

When this happens in adult love relationships, the balance is upset and the relationship becomes removed from reality. It is crucial for Love

Addicts not to abandon themselves but to maintain the reality of their personality and autonomy.

An inappropriate balance in the levels of emotional energy between child and parent (or other parental figure) is one of the most important factors that lead to Love Addiction. In a healthy relationship between a child and his or her parental figure the child receives nurturing love. This is shown by meeting a child's needs emotionally and practically and being able to respond to the child appropriately as the child develops into adolescence.

The child is able to learn gradually about relationships and what is needed to maintain them appropriately. Time will enable a child to make healthy decisions from the choices available to him or her. Without sufficient time or ability to manage the levels of energy spent on relationships, the child may hasten his or her decision process, thus reducing his or her choices. If the parent or parental figure is needy, the child learns quickly to respond in an attempt to ease the adult's stress level. As the pattern persists, the child delivers quicker and quicker. The process depletes the child's energy and can lead to the child withdrawing into isolation and low mood. Effectively, the imbalance of energy from child to adult elevates the adult to a higher power status, while the child has learned to abandon him/herself in the process.

If you are a Love Addict you will gain important insight into your adult relationships by observing the energy levels that you needed to devote to your parents (or parental figures) in order to maintain the relationship. It is likely that a similar pattern of energy expenditure plays out in your adult relationships.

Excessive daydreaming

The Love Addict will have experienced a rejection or abandonment either emotionally or physically from the parental figure, leading to feelings of loss and sadness. The child may find ways to soothe these immensely painful feelings. The child, the future Love Addict, will develop her skills of day dreaming or fantasising as a method of concealing the reality of being alone or feeling abandoned. Excessive levels of energy may be spent day dreaming or fantasizing in order to help relieve the sadness and the shame of feeling unlovable by the parent or caregiver. The sadness can prove overwhelming as the realisation of the loss of love dawns.

Attempting to cover up our feelings can be exhausting and may lead to confusion of what our feelings really are. For the Love Addict withdrawal into an isolated state will help relieve the drain of energy: this vital coping skill is designed to replenish energy, but, unfortunately, it diminishes still further the child's sense of self. Isolation also provides more time to continue daydreaming and fantasizing. A mistrust of the self forms and harmful thinking patterns may begin to develop – that they are not likeable or good enough, for example. An uncomfortable and paradoxical dynamic of 'I want so much to be loved' and 'You wouldn't love me if you knew me' develops. The fantasy of how love should be keeps replaying, while, simultaneously, the belief of not being good enough to receive love becomes entrenched. The result is an emotional trap.

Coping alone

The child that has learnt to withdraw and isolate him/herself as a coping skill may find that he or she suffers low mood together with low energy. Isolation for extended periods of time can lead to depression, which may prove to be a lifelong consequence for the Love Addict. The loss of sense of self provides a flimsy, unstable platform for the development of healthy self-esteem. Love Addicts typically gain self-esteem through their relationships rather than a sense of their own worth – for example, 'My husband is a consultant physician' or 'My partner owns his or her own company'. This is how Love Addicts attempt to win self worth and support a diminished self-esteem.

Once the Love Addict reaches adulthood and begins a love relationship, the fantasy of being loved truly, madly, deeply may engender a feeling of entitlement. The Love Addict has waited a long time to be taken care of by her knight in shining armour and to have all her emotional and practical needs met. This causes an imbalance of energy and emotional effort within the relationship. The other person in the relationship may feel that he is not being acknowledged and that the work he puts into the relationship is being taken for granted. The giving and caring within a relationship need to resonate around the 50-50 mark – in other words, relationships demand give and take, except, naturally, when a particularly stressful life event demands more nurturing of one partner than the other.

One of my clients wanted her knight in shining armour to be dazzled by her and effectively to put her on a pedestal. He would be safe, secure and famous; consequently, other people would notice her and she would gain esteem. It proved devastatingly disappointing for her, as, eventually, each knight in shining armour turned out to be a human being and unable to rescue her from the world. Reality always hit with a painful crash.

The parental figure may be present but emotionally unavailable to care for the child. Alternatively, the child may invest exhausting amounts of energy in the relationship with the major caregiver that is, by definition, limited: for example, the adult may be absent due to work commitments or military service. The effect, however, is the same: the child puts into the relationship an excessive energy that is not returned. The child's needs are not met and the child, consequently, experiences anxiety or high stress levels.

The adult Love Addict has, typically, experienced a parental relationship that is neglectful of emotional energy. Either one of the parents or parental figures may have abandoned the child physically or emotionally, perhaps unintentionally, but the results can, nevertheless, prove emotionally scarring.

Excessive demands upon the child

When a love imbalance occurs such as a child experiencing the absence of one parental figure, the child may find him/herself attempting to compensate for the emotional imbalance with the other parental figure. This is not necessarily a voluntary response, although the child may offer his/her services willingly. The child may find him/herself emotionally or physically meeting the needs of the remaining caregiver and, in some cases, taking on the role of the missing partner. Excessive energy is required from the child to fill such a role. The child, who is vulnerable and desperate for approval, may find that the special relationship with the adult offers him/her a reassurance of self-worth. It may well relieve the stress of feeling rejected by the other parental figure.

The child may invest in a supporting role to gain attention and acceptance at a deep level. An overly close or co-dependent relationship forms between child and adult. This is known as an enmeshed relationship. The child finds it difficult to distinguish where their self ends and the self of the other person begins. Individual boundaries blur, leading to confusion for the child about their identity as they grow into adulthood. They suffer a sense of not knowing who they are.

Enmeshment and abandonment may influence the child's emotional development toward love addiction and love avoidance. The Love Avoidant or commitment-phobic person may originate in the enmeshed parental relationship. It is common to find that a Love Addict will also show traits of Love Avoidance, a need for separation in order to replenish emotional energy levels. Abandonment is traumatic for a child. Withholding love, and the energy it provides, becomes emotionally disabling. The level of stress caused by abandonment can be relentlessly draining as the child struggles to develop emotionally.

How we respond to enmeshment and abandonment

When a person's emotional needs remain unmet, responses such as depression and anger typically result.

Depression

Depression may occur at any time as a response to emotionally painful issues. Many love-addicted clients refer to their feelings of anger as they start to acknowledge their depressed state and begin to identify their deeper feelings. This usually happens after they have witnessed their own denial. Then they can begin to explore their feelings of grief. Denial is a useful coping mechanism that protects us from pain and rejection. Letting go of denial – and starting to admit deep feelings – produces a profound sense of loss and grief. Denial, anger, grief, sadness and depression are all closely linked and each overlapping stage demands to be accepted.

Signs of depression include:

- losing one's zest for life
- difficulty in sleeping
- waking early in the morning
- changes in appetite – eating either more or less than usual
- apathy
- poor concentration
- despair
- suicidal feelings

Unexpressed anger often leads to depression. It is understandable that any child who is deprived of what is naturally his/hers – namely, love and being cared for – will feel anger. If that anger is internalised and withheld for long periods of time, depression may be the only way of dealing with the pain. A depressed person will often have no energy and feel too tired to attend to the basic tasks of self-care such as personal hygiene.

Anger

Social laws dictate that anger should be controlled. However, anger is as healthy an emotion as joy or passion, provided that people learn how to experience and express their anger appropriately. Newspapers are full of stories of revenge and uncontrolled anger, because some people cannot express their anger in an appropriate way.

Anger needs to be acknowledged and expressed: one of its purposes is to enable us to recognise a threat or potential violation and respond quickly to that threat. Anger signifies to the other person how we feel.

Anger can act as a defence, and defence is something that a person with low self-esteem or someone who is codependent will find difficult to achieve. Codependence is a survival mechanism that people use in order to feel better about themselves: pleasing others supports the codependent's distorted sense of self-esteem (see Chapter 11). Anger is difficult for codependents to express and to tolerate, for they often perceive anger as disapproval. Codependents are anxious to receive approval from others: it is one of the ways in which they define themselves and build their self-esteem. While it may sometimes be advisable to delay an expression of anger, it is always best, eventually, to acknowledge and express it appropriately. Healthy ways of expressing anger are described at the end of this chapter.

Learning to love oneself

Information such as the memory of joyful and familiar comfortable feelings is imprinted on the template formed in our early development. As we grow older and begin to form adult love relationships, we use the information stored within us to regain pleasurable memories, a kind of memory recall system. Where the parental figure or caretaker forming the primary relationship did not show the child love, the child will adapt his experience of love into a normalised understanding of what love is. At a biophysical level the stress that is experienced by the child can be immense and increases the levels of cortisol in the body. The higher our levels of cortisol, the more intense we become as the anxiety and stress within us rise: anxiety and stress about being abandoned or rejected. The need to calm and soothe in some way to reduce the stress and anxiety is a necessary coping strategy. Coping skills include daydreaming/fantasy, image obsession, eating disorders, sex – any number of ways in which stress can be reduced.

Each of these may seem like a strange and unwise way of coping and of course that is correct, only the intention is to achieve calm and relax from the primary stress – isolation and loneliness. Thinking styles connected to these overwhelming fears may well lead to harmful thinking patterns that carry the message of 'If I am not lovable I will not be taken care of. If I am not taken care of then I will die'. It makes sense to understand that a person carrying around this type of thinking pattern will have thoughts of self-hatred.

An attempt in later love relationships may replay early childhood experiences and confuse love relationships with abusive behaviours or acting out with addictions, attempting to calm or soothe the anxiety of the original abandonment. For example, in a situation where a child witnessed abusive behaviour either verbally or physically the child is likely to expect that this type of behaviour within a love relationship is acceptable. The child has to normalise his or her early life experience in order to survive it. By thinking that an abusive behaviour is acceptable or normal they may come to think they have permission to behave that way themselves. It is difficult for an abusive person to understand that what they are saying or doing is abusive if they have not interpreted it that way during their early developmental years. To those that have initially experienced such love relationships through their parental figures or caretakers what they are doing is 'loving' even if they are in fact being abusive.

How we perceive love relationships

We need to be able to determine whether what we experienced as a child was in fact love. Was it care? Was it positive attention? Was it nurturing? If it was a positive experience, then the primary love relationship was healthy. The child who experiences this type of love may grow into adulthood being able to identify other loving relationships: he/she will know how to receive love and therefore give healthy love.

For people who do not experience such a balanced level of care and attention relationships are much harder. In particular, the difficulties for the Love Addict, whose childhood was deprived of love by a significant relationship or parental figure, and who will have had an experience that was one of abandonment, rejection and isolation, may prove almost insurmountable. Self-discovery, together with the help of a qualified counsellor, will help.

Healthy ways of expressing anger

We have seen that depression and anger may surface from buried feelings of neglect, sadness and grief. The feelings of anger – because we did not receive what we so wanted and needed in our childhood – can build and build and, at certain trigger points, explode in the adult love relationship. Resentments towards a love partner in adult life may therefore have little to do with that person, but more to do with what that person symbolises. A Love Addict may eventually engage with a partner who will be subjected to suffering all the hurt and pain experienced by the Love Addict in childhood. This is a case of acting out anger and rage upon our love partner. The long buried feelings still hurt and we need to express, somehow, those feelings. To do this constructively, we may decide to embark upon self-help and professional therapy.

Self-help

First, you will find it helpful to develop the right breathing technique. Breathe in into your diaphragm/belly and fill your lungs with oxygen. Take it slowly and gently. Even more slowly, gently let the air out. This is an effective way of de-stressing the body. Always do this when you find that your anger is making you feel uncomfortable. If you still feel uncomfortable, talk to a professional counsellor or therapist, via your GP, in order to help you.

Remember, first, how your parental figures expressed their anger:
- ♥ When I was a child, when Mum got angry she would…
- ♥ When I was a child, when Dad got angry he would…
- ♥ When I was a child, when Grandfather got angry he would…
- ♥ When I was a child and I got angry, I would…

Explore your anger by writing about it. 'I am angry because…' This enables you to identify more specifically what your issues may be and to express them privately. Sometimes when anger is experienced at a physical level – in churning stomach, headache, dizziness, shortness of breath, for example – we need to find ways of expressing the emotion in order to let go of the built-up tension and stress. Some suggestions are:

- ♥ Take a towel and twist it tightly, feeling the tension in the fists and body slowly ebb away, biting the towel, if necessary, in order to release the energy of that anger from the jaw.
- ♥ Take a trip to an isolated place and shout and shout as loudly as you can. Feel the release as the energy dissipates.
- ♥ Throwing pebbles into water – by the river or the sea – acts as a conduit for the energy of anger.
- ♥ Engage in any kind of sport as an effective means of releasing anger and stress. You may choose from squash, football, tennis, swimming, for example. Be aware as you engage in your activity that you should focus on letting your anger feelings out.
- ♥ Pound your pillows. Use your body to release the tension that lies within.
- ♥ Bold, rhythmic music, played as loud as you can, but with due consideration for your neighbours.
- ♥ Write it all out – write and write and write until you can write no more. Describe how you feel in your body and in your mind. Describe the issues that you believe are making you angry. Now look at the list and explore how you may resolve each one, taking the first tiny steps towards balance and recovery.

Overcoming depressive moods

To break free from depressive moods we need to nurture ourselves and re-learn how to feel joy. This can prove very difficult when battling depression and necessitates a shift in our emotional environment. (Of course, if depression is severe, professional medical help will be needed.)

Helpful tools to improve energy levels and keep depression at bay include:

- ❤ Reaching out to others. Surround yourself with safe people – such as reliable, old friends and family – that you can share with in times of need. Seek out those people who will give you affirming reassurances that you're all right.
- ❤ Put a regular exercise regime in place, of some 20–30 minutes a day on up to three days of the week, choosing from gentle walks, a bicycle ride, a swim, a run, a yoga class, or a round of golf.
- ❤ Concentrate on eating regular healthy meals, starting with a good sustaining breakfast. Be sure to drink plenty of water.
- ❤ Do not let yourself become isolated, home alone. Withdrawal is one of depression's best friends.
- ❤ Avoid reading excessively and watching too much TV, both of which can isolate and separate you from healthy interaction with neighbours, friends, colleagues and family.

KEY POINTS
- ❤ The more healthy energy you spend the better you will feel
- ❤ Devoting excessive energy to a parent, in the process known as enmeshment, may damage the child in later adult relationships
- ❤ Daydreaming may be a response to parental abandonment and isolation
- ❤ Fantasising is an unhealthy and debilitating, inappropriate behaviour in adulthood
- ❤ A child will creatively adapt to his emotional environment
- ❤ The child learns to compensate for unmet needs
- ❤ Anger needs to be expressed, appropriately.

Chapter
4

Compassion in Loss

Grieving for the loss of love is an important phase in recovery from Love Addiction and from the powerlessness that we suffer in a futile attempt to relieve a childhood loss of love and attention. The intensity of the loss is very similar to the loss we feel with the death of a loved one. It is a sense of loss of self, the self being the way we see ourselves in the world, how we define ourselves and how we give meaning to our lives. The self has been damaged and a fundamental part of healthy development disrupted.

We need to treat and heal the symptoms of the loss. A basic, instinctive human need was not met and so the child, in adulthood, may attempt to fulfil that basic need by seeking love at almost any cost. It is a destructive loop for the Love Addict, who seeks, insatiably, the missing element: that of love.

Why we need to forgive

Compassion for ourselves is essential in order to heal our inner pain. We need to develop compassion and forgiveness for everything that we may have done in order to achieve peace and acceptance, qualities that are harmonious with healthy love. While we are accountable for our actions in the pursuit for love, including actions that may have been destructive to others, we may remain in a state of shame and low self-esteem until we develop a reasonable compassion and self-forgiveness for our deeds. The ideal is to achieve a balanced compassion without leaning towards self-pity and the victim mode. If you experience self-pity, and an inclination to wallow in your pain, you may need to seek professional assistance in order to help you move forward, address the imbalance and achieve a true compassion initially for yourself and, later, for others, as a vital stage of your healing process.

The parental figure's inability to fulfil childhood needs may have derived from their own emotional pain and disturbance, which will have influenced them in any nurturing role. It does not necessarily mean that they are, or were, bad people; only that they may have done things that may have been inappropriate at the time. Recovery is not about blame. Blame serves only to obscure the truth and keep you stuck emotionally. We may choose to forgive them at another, later, stage when it is appropriate for us. We can heal our wounds and build new loving relationships with whom we choose after we have worked upon our own recovery. This vital healing journey will empower us to make appropriate choices for ourselves at each stage of our lives.

The inner child

Effective recovery is enhanced when we recognise the neediness of our 'child within', commonly known as the 'inner child'. People who have experienced a childhood loss of love and attention from their chief caregiver may suffer a constant, profound sense of grief. This lurking sense of grief may symbolise a yearning for the relationship that could have been. (The inner child is discussed more fully in Chapter 5: *The burden of shame*.)

The Love Addict receives a clear message that underpins the distorted belief that 'I need someone to take care of me and I will not survive if I am alone.' In my case, my father's own issues disrupted my early attachment to him and I was unable to heal the pain I felt from him. Although unspoken, my father's message to me – that I was unlovable – was clear. My need for his love was great and it engendered my belief that only he, or a love like his, would heal my pain. I became emotionally needy for men.

Carried shame

I was deeply ashamed of being considered unacceptable and unworthy of love. I was, in effect, carrying my father's shame, known as carried or toxic shame. (See Chapter 5: *The burden of shame.*) My shame derived from my father's feelings of shame, which, in turn, originated with his own issues. He and my mother had a tempestuous relationship in which each sought to gain power over the other in order to pre-empt the threat of abandonment. Sex was the way in which they sought this power. My mother had suspected my father of having affairs and, in her own need to gain power within their relationship, she led him to suspect that I was not his child. My mother kept me close to her as I represented emotional value to her; in this way, her own insecurities contributed to my sense of carried shame – her shame being transferred to me – and reinforced the message I received from my father. Because I felt unlovable, I would go to extremes to prove the opposite. I have memories of climbing all over my father when I was a child of about four or five, trying desperately, in vain, to win his attention and his affection, to be rewarded only with profound irritation on his part. This shows how a desperate need for love can initiate a pattern of compulsive behaviours in the Love Addict; they feel compelled, as adults, to try to gain – repeatedly – the missing childhood experience of love satisfaction, resulting in Love Addiction.

Coping strategies

Interestingly, the Love Addict may be very capable and successful, a high achiever when outside of a love relationship; however, when in a love relationship, healthy functioning goes awry and all common sense evaporates as her excess energy refocuses on the goal of love rather than the goal of achievement. We Love Addicts need to let go of the fantasy that protected us in the past and realise that this is an inappropriate protection skill for a healthy, functioning adult. It is important at the same time to honour our childhood coping skills. Those that helped protect me from that childhood reality would be to remain silent and withdraw and isolate myself. I was considered to be peaceful and content as a child. I would play on my own in my bedroom for hours, fantasising with my dolls to create the perfect life in which I could lose myself. Or I would take myself off on my bicycle exploring, once again daydreaming to get me through my pain.

I would daydream for hours at school, gazing through the window, losing myself in a world outside the classroom. I remember one of my teachers asking me why I had such a worried look on my face. The reality was that I was in emotional pain, confused and worried. As a therapist I sometimes look at the physical appearance of a client and guess the age or the expression that the client holds in their body. It is my experience that the body holds or becomes stuck at a traumatic stage or age of development. With a gentle approach, at a stage later in therapy, the client may wish to explore these observations.

From isolation to intimacy

I can understand why I looked worried and can appreciate that fantasising helped me cope with the enormity of my traumatic childhood experience, the loss of love. I honour that part of me that knew how to ease my pain and see me through a troubled time. However, it is vitally important to accept that while such skills may have been useful in the past, it is not useful now to isolate or withdraw from people and stop from sharing thoughts and truths, particularly in a loving and intimate relationship. In fact, withdrawal and isolation are two important factors that impede our ability to experience intimacy within relationships. Those behaviours kept me from living in spontaneity and authenticity. By becoming aware, through my own therapy, of my patterns and behaviours and distorted thinking styles, I have been able to break free from the coping skills learned in childhood. I have become more emotionally available and less fearful of losing love and, gradually, I have become less needy in love relationships. Because I am aware of the speed with which I can return to old patterns, however, I need to remain vigilant and retain my awareness by continuing with self-development. Awareness and self-development can be a tiring journey at times, but one that I would recommend anyone in an addiction state to continue.

Learning to communicate with my father

An important catalyst for the shift from childhood coping skills to adult awareness and understanding came as a result of writing a letter to my father. The letter was direct and, on reflection, not accurate at all. I had not spoken to him for several years. His call came one morning; his anger bellowed down the phone, as he demanded to speak with me. I put in place my first ever boundary with him, telling him that I was not able to talk with him at that time. I had children to prepare for school and I wanted my full concentration for our conversation. I suggested a later time to have our chat; this proved to be a turning point in our relationship, as I found my ability to face my father's anger and ask for what I needed. My father was agreeable and not as angry as I had thought he would be. The first boundary I had set exerted a profound effect on me, as I was not used to having my needs met and self-empowerment was not a usual experience for me. (See also Chapter 9: *Recognising boundaries in relationships*.)

We agreed a lunch date for later in the week. We met at his house and he had arranged a lunch for me. We were able to talk for the first time in our lives with honesty and love. It was the first time he had told me that he loved me and that he was sorry for the way he had treated me in the past. We hugged and began a new understanding of each other. It was a breakthrough and we did not look back thereafter. My father has since passed away and I am forever thankful for our move towards intimacy and love.

Facing the truth

How we coped as a child and the skills we used to deal with each situation need to be honoured. We also need to understand that they may not be appropriate in a healthy, functioning adult and that we need to mature. The skills we learned not only protected us from unacceptable truths but also protected our caregivers from our anger and negative feelings. We naturally feel guilty if we say bad things about our parents or those who have looked after us. So, yet again, we abandon ourselves by denying our feelings in order to protect others and keep them emotionally comfortable. This is a classic sign of codependence (see Chapter 11: *Interdependence within love*).

By fantasising that things weren't so bad and escaping the reality through fantasy, we create a protective shell around our caregivers as well as ourselves. The fear of upsetting the parental figure may explain why it is so difficult for some people to acknowledge their truth. Recalling our childhood years as happy appears to be the use of denial as a psychological protection. However, acknowledging the truth as it appeared to us at the time is crucial to recovery.

Looking for patterns

The primary relationship between child and caregiver forms the basis of the child's thinking and behaviour. This leads in turn to how we as adults form emotional relationships. Look for what a person represents or symbolises in the adult relationship in order to draw some parallels between the adult relationship and the primary love relationship. You may observe similar characteristics or parallels in both. The childhood relationship may be a relationship formed between the child and parents, grandparents, childcare workers, neighbours, teachers or any adult caregivers. If trauma or shame exists in any important relationship in our formative years, we are likely to perpetuate such issues in adult life.

We can protect ourselves from emotional pain and Love Addiction if we understand that the attraction into a significant adult relationship may resemble the unresolved parental relationship in childhood, the relationship in which the child's emotional needs were abandoned.

Forgiving myself

You may ask what chance do we have of resolution and success in love relationships if we were traumatised at an early age by love deprivation. It took me some time to understand that I was not to blame for the choices I had made in the past: I had been ashamed of my failed relationships and thought that they were attributable to my poor judgment. However, as an adult I am accountable for my choices in life. I have undertaken several years of therapy to guide and support me in my quest for reality: what has become clear is that I did not understand relationship dysfunction and relationship cycles to the degree that I needed. If I could understand what I was doing that negatively affected my relationships, I would be able to modify my thoughts and behaviours to enable me to relate in a healthy way to my partner. If I could bring some sense into what at that time seemed senseless, I would have a chance of succeeding in a love relationship. My symptoms of grief and pain were not being treated, but that has now changed, thanks to the work carried out by relationship experts such as Pia Mellody.

Moving forward from grief to compassion

These steps will enable you to access the empathy and compassion for your 'child within' and help you to resolve the emotional pain:

❤ Write a letter to the parent or caregiver who holds so much pain for you. The letter does not have to be posted; its purpose is to process your feelings.

♥ Explain what you needed from him/her in the way of emotional energy, be it love, support or attention, that was important for you at that time.

♥ Explain what you did receive from that person in place of what was needed and describe how that felt at the time.

♥ Describe how the loss of what you needed has manifested itself in your life today.

♥ If you feel that you are at a stage of being able to forgive, explain that you understand that this part of your childhood development can never return and that you have let go of the loss and now hold on to the future, living in the moment, and cherish yourself in the course of each day.

♥ Write about your understanding of the cause of the pain. Perhaps it was learned behaviour from previous generations. If appropriate, describe your compassion for them.

♥ Write about your sadness and feelings for any significant adult relationship you have engaged with that has ended with pain and grief.

♥ Write about the loss of the dreams you may have held for the future. Those dreams may have involved other people or perhaps they were your personal dreams that changed for reasons beyond your control.

♥ Forgiveness is the first step to loving oneself. Feeling a genuine compassion for ourselves is essential in our journey of healing our emotional wounds.

KEY POINTS

♥ Compassion is a vital part of healing your emotional pain
♥ Recognising your inner child enables compassion
♥ The search for personal truth is essential for recovery
♥ Letting go enables us to move forward.

Chapter
5

The Burden of Shame

We suffer shame as a result of emotional traumatic experiences and messages given by the norms of society. These may include older generation or educational or spiritual facilities. This chapter is concerned with trauma that leads to shame, carried shame (generational or inherited shame), how shame is expressed and how to recognise and express one's inner shame. Both shame and guilt signify a loss of dignity and a loss of self: guilt is the feeling that signifies to us we have done something that violates our own belief system. In other words, 'I feel guilty because I have done something bad'. Shame is a more deeply internalised message that makes someone feel that 'I am a bad person', rather than 'I have done something bad'. Shame is a powerful and painful feeling caused by a strong sense of feeling exposed. Both shame and guilt can engender bodily reactions as well as emotions.

Shame originates as a protection. In other words, at the earliest time when shame began it may have initiated a need to withdraw to a safer environment or remain silent. As a child this may be a healthy survival response. For example, 'If I speak people may think I'm stupid; at least that's what my Dad told me, so I will keep quiet.' Sadly, for those who have not experienced a healthily functioning family system, the protective behaviour stays in place inappropriately and remains embedded in the psyche throughout development instead of moving through various stages of maturity, and for some the message replays itself in adulthood. The further consequences of this thinking may inhibit a person's career, relationships and potential.

Some causes of shame

Abandonment and rejection are traumatic for any child. Trauma comprises a normal set of reactions to abnormal events; the effects upon our biochemistry are stimulated either by external reactions or internal thoughts. Given this template of early life experience, which forms the building blocks of development, the child integrates the traumatic information into her thinking and behaviour patterns. Here is an example of trauma for a three-year old when she was separated by accident from her mother:

> "The lift was full of people and my mummy was with me. I was close to the doors and at some stage the doors opened. I walked through the doors into a large open space. It was dark, damp, smelly, cold, and empty except for cars. I tried to find my mummy but I couldn't see her anywhere, the doors had shut and I was alone. I remember crying and feeling terrified. I still have a problem with car parks today."

This example shows how an innocent incident can be interpreted as terrifying and begin a template for the child to experience fear or threat within a given set of circumstances. It is important to remember that each of us has our own interpretation of what signifies fear or threat, depending on our experiences. As the above example illustrates, this child may have begun to develop fears of abandonment and a terror of being alone since the time of this experience. If similar experiences happened after that time she may also have easily developed a hyper-vigilance for abandonment or being left alone unexpectedly.

The intensity of fear and threat create a chemical reaction in the brain. If the trauma wound is sufficiently deep and terrifying, the body's chemical make-up alters and the system becomes heightened into an alarm state, of never feeling safe. The body is waiting now, alert, for the pain and hurt to re-occur, which leads to a biochemical change in the brain. The more intense the threat is, the more the brain is flooded with neurochemicals. This process leads to chemical overloading of the neuropathway into the brain. This overload is called 'satiation'. It tells us whether we have been satisfied or not, a kind of measurement of satisfaction. Substances and behaviours can calm, relax and create electrochemical reactions in the brain that reduce the heightened anxiety. When the source of the fear goes away, the chemicals subside and satiation will adjust to a normalised level. The person may experience a craving for the biochemical effect they have experienced, and a need to reach a level of satisfaction can occur, and this craving can lead to addiction.

The person that has been emotionally traumatised may become attached to or crave the person, or people similar to the person, that caused the trauma. The individual may even take on the blame, emphasising distorted thinking regarding who is responsible for what. Attachments to such toxic relationships cause a distrust of the individual's own judgment, as his/her reality has become distorted to such an extent s/he cannot see the risks of such attachments. Once in a state of readiness for trauma, the individual doesn't notice the grieving process s/he is suffering, as, by now, part of her/him – emotionally – has died. A need to shut down from the pain can happen as a way of coping with the awful event. The person adapts to cope with the pain, shock, disbelief and sadness of grief and sometimes denial may be the way that the self is protected from trauma. By making this adaptation, the individual has learned to abandon himself or herself. This represents the ultimate trauma, the loss of self.

Loss may compel the adult Love Addict to make choices that lead to further experiences of abandonment, this time by each of her love partners. Here's how it works: the child's terrifying experience may lead to compensating behaviours for her fears of being left alone. It may be that her anxiety levels rise when she is alone, or alone in a car park, or finds herself in a crowded lift, as described in the earlier example. To compensate and protect herself from such events, she may become overly needy or clingy in relationships because the person she lost, temporarily, during that early life experience, was her mother, with whom she would have had a very powerful, primary, dependent love relationship. The fear may replay itself in other significant relationships like a re-enactment: for example, with women she may idolize them or become needy and anxious if she thinks or interprets that she is being rejected or abandoned by them.

If the original trauma was abandonment and separation from the mother, as in the car park example, she may even create strategies such as avoiding taking elevators, perhaps making sure she has ground floor reservations in hotels and restaurants. She may choose to take the stairs whatever the number of floors she needs to reach.

In my own example, I became clingy, relentlessly trying to gain my father's love and approval. This behaviour pattern developed into adult love relationships with men which went awry. As an adult, I replayed the need for approval and love from each successive love partner.

I am lovable

Stuck in this relentless cycle, I found achieving love was impossible. No matter how much I was told and each partner tried to show me, I was unable to accept the information as truth – I did not trust in being loved. I had developed the belief that I was not worthy of love. Relief from this painful condition came only when I was able to achieve a balanced belief in myself, through using vital tools that were appropriate to my own needs, such as boundaries for protection and boundaries to protect others from me. (See Chapter 9: *Recognising boundaries in relationships*.) I also used affirmations to develop a healthy inner affirming voice, instead of the one that told me I was 'never up to the mark', 'never good enough', 'not worthy'. I learned to replace negative messages with positive ones that told me 'I am enough' and that 'I am valuable', that 'I am lovable', 'I am worthwhile'.

I learned to calm the internal distress of my inner child, thinking I was unworthy of love or not sufficiently valuable to be loved, by re-parenting my inner child: this is an important part of therapeutic work that reassures our inner self, the child within, that the pain no longer needs to exist the way that it did when we were young, defenceless and dependent on our parental figure. As an adult, one no longer needs to believe in being dependent on another person or in being defenceless in the world.

The moving piece of work that follows is by a client who wrote to her inner child. This enabled her to step forward and acknowledge what her feelings of distress were linked to, which, in her case, was the experience of decades of being bullied.

'To my inner child'

I would like to tell her I'm so sorry I ignored her for so long. I pretended I couldn't see her and that she wasn't there but maybe it was just that she was hiding and I didn't want to look. Now I'll always try and look for her and promise to try to be kind and quiet with her.

When she's panicky and scared I want to hold her by the hand and tell her how wonderful she is, how amazingly special and unique... her eyes hiding behind a long fringe watching everything. When she's scared I want to smooth her hair down and speak softly and quietly to her. I want to tell her that it's OK and I won't leave her, that we can do it together. That I'll make sure she's safe.

I'd like to entice her out of her safe shell, a little hermit crab, and say that it's OK to have fun and be silly, that she needn't be scared because I'll be here to protect her. I want to show her that we can blow over the bullies with one big breath; watch how they fall over, they're made of nothing, bits of paper. I want to tell her that she does everything so beautifully, that she enchants people without even knowing it. I want to fill her head with unconditional praise so that it just comes tumbling out.

I want to teach her how to look after herself, how to stand tall when people are unkind and how to leave any situation she wants to. I also want to teach her how to say anything that's on her mind, no matter who it's about, that all thoughts and feelings are good because they're hers. I want to show her how to be proud about everything she does so that she will hold up the things that she makes, hold them next to her face and grin with glee because she's delighted with something that's hers. So I will congratulate her over and over on all her achievements and remind her of them when things are difficult.

I would like to show her how to run free and do as she pleases. To put her own needs first, and, only once they are met, to look to others. I'll show her how to cock a snoop at convention and manners and be merry and reckless and not bother with whether it suits other people or not. To be like the crazy rabbit that became a fox – when he walks into a room and doesn't like the people in it, he goes straight to the nearest corner and pisses in it. And we cheer.

I want to tell her how very beautiful she is, how people envy her but don't know how to express it so sometimes they're unkind. I want to tell her that in her I see this steely and quiet determination that will see her through all the bad stuff. That she's strong enough to take on the world; she just needs to believe it. So I'll tell her again and again until she does.

And most of all I want to tell her how proud I am of her. That she is a joy to know, the most beautiful person I know and I will love her forever with no ifs and buts. I will tell her that the world is lucky to have her. And I will hug her and pick her up and spin her over my head so that she screams with laughter and love.

In this example the client identifies how she feels when something bad happens, hiding behind her fringe when she felt scared, and how external influences had forced her to obey convention and ignore her spontaneous yearning to be allowed to come through and play and laugh as a child wants and needs to do. She was able to acknowledge how her traumatised experience of childhood had trained her to put other people's needs and wants first, ignoring her own. This is classic codependent behaviour. Through working on her inner child, by means of re-parenting, she was able to attend to her own needs and wants appropriately, especially by using calming techniques such as affirmations.

Shedding trauma and shame

In my own case I worked on defining myself, working out who I was, rather than accepting myself as a blur of people-pleasing in order to keep others comfortable and ultimately abandoning myself. Practising this new way of thinking was hard to do. It is necessary to regard the self as a priority: making oneself a priority can be a very uncomfortable and challenging task for the codependent. Gradually, I began to gain self-esteem; I gradually became less in need of a love relationship to define who I was, to give me value and to keep me comfortable in my dysfunctional patterns.

Traumatic experiences can affect our very being to such a degree that they may replay themselves time after time: this is known as trauma repetition (Carnes 1997) in which the objective of repeating the cycle of trauma is to bring about resolution of the original trauma and relief from the original emotional pain. For example, the little girl in the case at the beginning of this chapter continued to be needy as an adult, attempting to compensate for the original trauma and its associated high levels of inner stress and anxiety. Some people remain stuck in this cyclic process of traumatic re-enactment for years, and some for their entire lives.

A series of traumatic events of low intensity can naturally lead to chronic trauma. The events may produce a lower intensity of stress, but the repetition may nevertheless produce a long-term effect. Such events may lead to chronic mild depression or to dysthymic depression. Dysthymic depression is characterised, essentially, by an almost daily depressed mood for at least two years and that mood never being absent longer than two consecutive months, but without the criteria for a major depression. Both chronic mild depression and dysthymic, or 'unipolar' depression describe a state in which someone is lacking in motivation, quietly angry at life, and has learned to accept the distress experienced. Dysthymic depression is like the feeling that, although you are functioning to full capacity, you are tired of life and you feel 'I'll never get it right'. There is an unspoken acceptance of failure and low expectation.

Obsessive repetition

A child who has tried, in vain, to gain recognition and attention from the parental figure, perhaps by attempting to 'get it right' or be perfect, may develop obsessive and repetitive behaviours. Addictive cycles exist within a perfectionist mindset. As with most compulsive cycles, they are progressive and any traumatic event, therefore, may become more and more deeply embedded within the psyche, building in its intensity.

The mind has the capacity to replay trauma events in our lives, depending on the stimulation; this is similar to post-traumatic stress disorder (PTSD), in which flashbacks are one of the important symptoms. This type of replay or repetition can have a serious effect upon the mind. It can also affect the body and we may react in physical ways, just as I did in my experience with Charles and my pathological grief response.

The Love Addict is desperate for the love she did not receive as a child, and it is in adult love relationships that this is likely to be revealed. She will typically obsess over finding a love relationship or, when in a love relationship, she may obsess over her love partner, as this significant style of relationship has been one of the main losses in her life. When we are preoccupied or intensely focused in one area, we are no longer present in the moment. The obsession will cause a distraction to life in the present and may further increase levels of stress and anxiety as life around us is ignored or neglected.

Alongside the loss of love, and of similar significance, is the loss of self, as mentioned earlier in this chapter. It is often said that we cannot love another if we don't know how to love ourselves. When things begin to go wrong within the relationship, there is often an unrealistic belief that the relationship will find its way back to how it was in the beginning. This belief may prove to be a driving force towards obsessive thoughts – that she can make love happen if only she does something to make it happen – and, typically, this is the message the child has interpreted from the early bonding experience. The driving, compulsive force may lead to the child learning to perform or achieve for the parent in some way in order to gain attention, or to the adult to seek that all-important love exchange. This learned behaviour often veers towards a need for perfection.

Abandonment and neglect from the caregiver can undermine the child's confidence in her ability to take care of her self. Thus, the distorted message to the child is that she will need someone to take care of her. 'I will not survive if I am alone.' This shaming message can affect our ability to manage our entire lives.

Generational shame

Shame that is passed down through families is known as generational shame (Bradshaw, 2006). If we trace our family back through the generations, we may be able to find some revealing information that may have contributed to the development of our personality. We may find information such as adultery, incest, suicide; addictions such as alcohol, drugs or sexual affairs; obsessive compulsions such as hoarding, cleanliness, perfectionism or gambling. Such information may be relevant and help us to understand better the generational influence that has added to our feelings of powerful and destructive shame.

Such generational disorders can create havoc and chaos and sometimes ruin lives. One client of mine reported that she would often medicate her emotional pain and anxiety by cleaning the house excessively. A compulsive cleaner may clean and clean, over and over, until their skin bleeds from exhaustion. (Obsessive cleaning may present as a need to have control over the home environment, making it safe and secure. This is likely to be compensating for an insecurity in the original home environment, emphasised through family messages.) Some extreme behaviours may be repeated until physical injury is sustained and, even at that point, the person may not acknowledge their high level of stress and ignore the need to seek help. I have seen this reported in the case of some sex addictions: for example, a person that masturbates excessively to seek comfort – until they cause themselves physical injury as the addiction progresses. Fantasies can be well hidden, although they may be highly dangerous as in some cases as they can shift from fantasy to enactment; for sex addiction the trail can be devastating with the increased risk of disease, stalking, expense, and separating from daily life. The consequences can be immense. From my experience of working in the field of sex addiction, this is particularly devastating, especially as the addiction can be regarded as a source of pride by the sufferer and peer group.

As I explained in Chapter 4: *Compassion in loss*, sex was one of the forms of currency within the relationship between my parents. It was used as a means of holding power over each other. My mother's own carried shame had her acting as a co-sex addict to my father, enabling him to continue acting out while she sought revenge by pretending that I was not his child. Co-sex addicts are driven to have sex in order to keep the attention or love of their partner, which is a way of hooking the other person, thus securing the relationship. Acting out is a term used to describe someone remaining active in his or her addictive behaviour. In my father's case, my mother's inability to confront her fears that her husband was having sex with other women enabled him to continue the sexual encounters. It was my mother's shame at being abandoned that supported my father's behaviour. To give a further example of generational shame, my mother's shame was passed to her by experiencing events that related to her own father's numerous affairs, resulting in him abandoning the family when she was aged eight.

I was able to make the link that my mother had also been abandoned by her father and sex had played a significant role in that scenario. Her mother had also used her power within her marriage to distance her husband from his daughters by separating several times and finally by divorcing him. Divorce makes sense to an adult in that position, although, to a young child, it may have a more powerful, emotional effect with the child experiencing rejection, abandonment and self-blame, leading to still more shame. A child does not yet have the emotional and intellectual capacity to be able to process such situations in the way that adults can.

On my father's side of the family there was also evidence of sex addiction and family secrets, which had profound effects on our family. My grandmother on my father's side, that is my father's mother, had had a sexual relationship with her stepson, my father's half brother (my uncle). The result was the birth of a child, who herself, later, had a child – the grandchild of my father's half-brother. The clandestine relationship was kept secret for decades and only exposed after the death of my uncle (my father's mother had died a few years previously). In my uncle's will he left his entire estate to his grandchild, thus dramatically exposing the secret and shame after his own death. It caused enormous distress and emotional pain within the family and even now the rift still exists.

It is difficult to grow up in surroundings where physical actions and expressions are, apparently, the way to communicate. It leaves interpretation of events open and the effects can be far reaching. As I write this book, more family history and generational shame has come to light and helps lend perspective to my own sense of shame: and this underlines the significance of writing as a way of processing and accepting personal issues.

Family history can help people struggling with emotional issues, who may think they themselves are responsible for distressing family events. As mentioned earlier, a distrust of own judgements often happens due to high levels of anxiety and trauma. So, search for your family secrets to help you realign your perspective. Perhaps an aunt or family friend may hold the key to your understanding and relieve you of family shame. Be discreet in your search as the object is to gain information rather than to add shame to family members who may have not embarked on a journey of self-development and may not wish to be confronted with such information. Some people may find facing such reality is far too disturbing.

Had I married my father?

Perhaps I had continued the generational pattern? I had married a man, the father of my two sons, who, I believe, was a sex addict. From my experience, he was also intellectually abusive, demeaning of me and physically aggressive. This became clear only during the first couple of years with him: somehow, I had married my father. So why did I continue with what appeared to me to be an abusive relationship? I struggled with this question for many years. Why was I unable to leave a relationship that was so clearly neither nurturing nor supportive but hostile? And why had I begun the process again in my relationship with Charles?

What I now understand, through the process of my recovery, is that I enabled my second husband to stay comfortable, continuing with his abusive behaviour. And, in turn, I also stayed comfortable in supporting him due to my relentless search for his approval and love. It seems so clear to me now, as I write this, and I hope it becomes clear to you and that you may be able to detect your own patterns of family shame and compulsive behaviours. The question I often ponder is how this has affected my two sons. The answer, I guess, lies in the future. As I work on my own recovery, I can happily say that the relationship I have with my sons is as open and as honest as possible. I do witness repetitions of old family patterns that are clearly not healthy for them, although I appreciate the fact that I am powerless over my relationship with them and the most I can do is offer them an awareness of our family secrets.

We will always need to be vigilant if we want to make healthy relationship choices in the future. It is sometimes enough to expose family secrets of depth to ourselves to have a positive effect in changing the family patterns and let them go in order to move forward and reduce inherited shame for future generations. The power of secrets is likely to diminish once they are exposed. This also happens with shame: once exposed, its power is reduced and the generational pattern loses strength. (You can find out more on reducing shame at the end of this chapter.)

Protecting my parents

A revealing observation came while working on this book. On reading the first draft I was asked by a colleague why I had not included more information about my childhood experience with Love Addiction and the experience with Charles. My reply was 'What would my mother say?' 'How about my Dad? What would he think?' It was a perfect example of me keeping the family comfortable and protecting my parents from shame and in so doing continuing the process. The aim is not to cause pain and suffering, rather it is to halt the dysfunction and emotional pain that otherwise journey from one generation to the next. After you have begun to progress on your path of recovery, it may be possible to combine your feelings of hurt and sadness with acceptance within your newly defined relationships towards your parental figures. If you wish and when you have processed sufficiently your feelings, you may find an opportunity to create a fresh, authentic relationship: a healthy and balanced one in which you gain empowerment. It is a process that requires time, sensitivity and compassion.

Addicted to sex

To return to the effects of shame, the Love Addict becomes so entranced in her love fantasy she cannot see the chaos, and sometimes the danger, around her. It is not unusual for a Love Addict to interpret sex as a sign of love while seeking love. Confusion between the two may play a major part in the relationship. Co-sex addiction may be a likely element. By tracing family patterns back through the generations, you may find that sex played a major part in relationships…maybe in the form of affairs outside the family or incestuously within it. Sex may have been ignored or thought of as a degrading act. Such messages hold a powerful energy when passed down through the generations. Such family secrets contribute to creating 'carried' shame or toxic shame. We may struggle with carried shame and confuse it with what we regard as our own sense of shame, particularly so if we continue the behaviours, as I did.

It is important to separate what is carried shame from what is not. This can be done through personal therapy or through researching our own past and using one of the self-development books concerned with carried shame. A list of recommended reading is to be found at the end of the book.

Exposing the shame demons

One client of mine wrote about her experience of shame and her relationship to it, which shows, powerfully, how destructive shame can be:

Dear Shame,

>*You make me feel so angry and frustrated how you trap me and prevent me from doing what I want or be who I want to be. You have held me back for so long I have got so confused about which is the true me and which is the true shame that I carry around like a black cloud over me. And, you know something, I'm just sick of it. I'm so tired of you making me feel so ashamed of myself that I feel like having to hide all the time. I want to hit you, I want to beat you up, I want to kill you but I can't because I have no visual image to aim all my hatred at, all my anger at, all my pain at. And, because I'm so confused about where I stop and you, that shame, begins, the only way I know to vent my anger is at myself because you make me feel like it's my fault. And there you keep me in this cycle of hating myself and I detest you for it and I hate you for trapping me. You make me feel so low, so little, so boring, so disgusting, so lonely that I don't have enough energy to realise that it is you that is making me feel like this and, even when I try to fight the thoughts you put in my head, I still hear your voice saying to me 'Maybe this is who I am and how I will always feel'. When I hear this I feel it would be easier to give in, accept what you are telling me and I do it because it is easier than trying to fight the ideas that you have planted in my mind for so long and I have allowed to grow and grow and overwhelm me. You fill me with jealousy because I am jealous of the people around me and how they seem to be enjoying life and seem to find it so easy to interact with people. I hate it how you cause this green-eyed monster to appear, as it makes me feel like I'm a horrible person and a poor excuse for a human being.*

>*I even look at people and see how they are getting on with their life and I don't know how they can do it because I am finding it so hard to get on with mine. I hate you, I want you to disappear, because I don't*

want to have these feelings any more. I want to be free from your grip on me because you are such a dirty, low, oppressive thing that doesn't even deserve to be alive. But, even when I write this, you are still confusing me by telling me that you are I and these are my true feelings. You are just such a cruel thing that keeps on confusing me, keeps on keeping me from talking to people, keeps me from going out and making friends, keeps me hiding in the dark, making me feel worthless. You just seem to control me and inhibit me and stop me from being individual. You have locked me up and to me you are the thing that can choose when to release me. You make me judge people and you make me think people judge me and say nasty things behind my back. And years ago this wouldn't have crept into my mind, but nowadays you are always creeping into my mind looking for my weakest spots. Judging. Feeding negative thoughts into my head, and when I sometimes realise what you are doing, I just want to kill you, destroy you, and remove any trace that you even existed. Shoot you, pour acid over you and make you dissolve like the poison you are so that you take with you the poison you feed me. I have a right to do what I want, be who I want to be and you have no right to be here. You just live off me like a parasite, sucking the life out of me.

This description shows, very powerfully, just how painful the shame experience can be. It overwhelmed and controlled this client's life, almost suffocating the spirit and the life force of the true person. To reduce the effects of toxic or carried shame, it is necessary to expose demons so that the power they once held will begin to diminish. Once you have exposed the demons I would encourage you to change the relationship you had with them; for example, the once fearful and overwhelming shame needs to be understood and related to with a more compassionate acknowledgement. This will alleviate the element of fear and provide the space for you to begin a new relationship with yourself. It is likely that your demons will visit you again at certain times but the new relationship you adopt towards those fearful times will lessen in their intensity and the time they once demanded reduces as you become stronger in your self belief. Positive affirmations will be most important to habitually remind yourself of the valuable person that you are and that you are enough just as you are. This is possibly the best and most effective way of improving self-value and self worth. It is a wonderful tool to use anywhere at any time.

My addictions have presented in the following sequence. I was carrying the burden of shame of first codependence, then Love Addiction, then Love Avoidance and finally co-sex addiction. Co-dependence was learned primarily to keep my mother comfortable and help her exert power over my father. This was her shame and belongs to her, even though it was handed down to her through her parents' generation. I feel compassion for myself and for my mother about this. Love Addiction developed due to the rejection, the lack of acceptance, and the lack of approval, value and love from my father. I have understood why and I have compassion for him. Love Avoidance played its part due to the enmeshed relationship I had with my mother, leading me to feeling suffocated when I am subject too much to somebody else's neediness. It has been a significant struggle for me to come to terms with my mother's enmeshment. (See also the previous chapter: *Compassion in loss.*) The final childhood stage of my carried shame, culminated in co-sex addiction. I picked up the silent exchange of the sexual charge within my parents' relationship, the consequence of which was my own co-sex addictive behaviour. The co-sex addict, like the codependent, keeps the sex addict or dependent comfortable by enabling them in their addiction or behaviour. I understand the generational pattern of how this behaviour came into play and I have compassion over this.

The breakthrough of discovering carried shame for me was when the relationship with Charles ended, abruptly, with his death. It left me plummeting downwards, ever downwards. My world had come crashing down and I needed to understand. I needed to find a sense of perspective on what seemed senseless at the time… I was confused. I was at the very bottom. The physical manifestation of my shame was focused for years mainly in my head, causing migraine, sometimes lasting for as many as five days, as well as stomach problems.

An emotional fog

It is valuable to combine emotional pain with physical signs for those who experience difficulty with understanding their feelings. I encourage exploration of the somatic experience by using the mind's eye to identify colour, shape, size, texture, and so on. It is an attempt to harmonise emotional and physical experience.

It is not surprising that I was confused and in pain. As I explored the visual element of my physical pain, I discovered that the colour sensation was black and the weight was heavily loaded, leaving me feeling useless. Experiencing a feeling of being useless further compounds low self-esteem and can often lead to depression if anger is not expressed appropriately. The codependent often finds it difficult to express anger or even feel comfortable in acknowledging it. I also felt unacceptable and defective for having a relationship with Charles who so clearly lied to me. The attraction that held the power for me to become so attached to Charles, a significant hook, was that I believed he showed me total approval and acceptance: and I interpreted this as love. This euphoric feeling left me blind to the reality of his lies and unable to observe any boundaries. The emotional fog was thick. I was vulnerable, hooked, and incapable of functioning in a healthy way. The hook was that of acceptance and approval, both of which I craved.

Recognising the core of your shame

Once we are able to identify our triggers or hooks, or the initial attraction, we can flag them up as we begin a new relationship or revive an old relationship in a new way. Our flags may be red and warn us that we can choose to turn away from those relationships that are too dangerous for us. Healthy choices lead to healthy lives.

Another tool for reducing shame is to begin to imagine it, the shame, in its physical state, for example, its colour, its texture, its size, its shape, its location and what message it gives us. This information can connect us to our unexpressed feelings. We need to identify what role shame has been playing and its powerful control over us. As you get to know your shame, you will be identifying your shame core. This is usually best done in the safe and secure atmosphere of a therapeutic relationship with a qualified practitioner. However, if you are able to find other appropriate support, there is no reason why you cannot do this therapeutic work yourself. Shifting the style of relationship with shame from fear to 'visitor' is essential in order to manage shame attacks. A list of exercises to help reduce shame can be found at the end of this chapter.

Some of my own triggers are disapproval from others and, also, social events that trigger a sense of diminishment or exposure in me. I can remember completely freezing up when expected to say something at a social event. My face would turn red and I would become hot and perspire, and my mind would go blank. I had internalised an experience early in my childhood that shamed me in public and would haunt me in my adult life. I was about four or five years old and my father had taken me into a milk bar where they also sold sweeties. I was relentless in wanting some sweeties, possibly seeking sugar to feel good around my father; eventually, he told me in a loud voice, in front of all the people in the milk bar, that he would pull down my pants and smack my bottom. I can still remember the feeling of utter shame. I wanted to disappear. I felt dreadful, ashamed, exposed and unworthy. That was a time when I felt unworthy of being in public: I carried that public shame around for too long and it had the power to keep me small and hidden.

Liberation

I see many clients with shaming experiences that keep them, in their view, small and invisible to the world. Perhaps the information Charles had given me about his extraordinary social status and lifestyle was a hook for me to achieve social acceptance. He was a very capable man in social situations and could capture a crowd in an instant.

If we keep ourselves small, we will never achieve authenticity. To blossom truly in our own beauty, just as a flower needs the sun to bloom, we need to reach for our own potential. Shame can hold us back from this process. But, by actively pushing the shame core outside of ourselves, where it belongs, separating it from ourselves and reducing its power over us, we will be able to function in a more balanced manner in all situations, without fear of a shame or panic attack. Carried shame is a powerful destructive force; you have the power and the right to give it up and send it back to its place of origin. You will find ways of sending original shame back to its rightful place at the end of this chapter.

As I have stated earlier, my own co-sex addiction was a behaviour that I had devised in order to experience a feeling of being valuable and loved, thus calming me. Clearly this was the result of carried shame brought to me through my generational family message as stated on pages 98–99. I had not understood the behaviour as anything other than 'normal' as it was a soothing mechanism that I had taken on board through the silent family message as acceptable.

Healthy shame, however, is an important element of the self that is present in order to remind us of what is acceptable and what is not. For example, if we take a day off work under the guise of sickness, otherwise known as 'pulling a sicky', the social moral boundary is betrayed and a sense of 'I've done something unacceptable' is understood, depending on the culture of your workplace, although the action may also be a soothing experience without it inducing an overwhelming sense of self-judgment.

Family secrets are such because nobody is talking about truth; there is a collective, often unrecognised, cover-up. Children are able to read the unspoken word very well and, in fact, the spoken word may not even be needed to convey the secret. As a consequence of the secrets, the chain is kept alive and so the secrets and the shame live on, nurturing a hive of disease. Like all infections, if they are not attended to promptly, they will erupt into a poisonous mess and create further problems, just as our family secret did in my own example. When we expose the truth, we allow in the light and secrets and shame will begin to lose their power. Likewise, if they are kept underground, they will grow in strength and power, feeding a web of more secrets and shame, leaving a potential for family break-ups and destruction. The more we permit secrets and shame to remain unexposed, the more the damage will affect our families for future generations.

This is the toxic chaos that lies behind problems, such as addictive behaviours, acting out, compulsive relationships and other dysfunctions. When we think we have complete freedom of choice to behave and act as we like, that perhaps we are in control of who we are, it may be beneficial to analyse the facts and see the reality of our situation. What generational shame and family secrets are you holding on to? How much does that negative energy affect your life today and your decisions? Perhaps we are bound in emotional chains, disabling us from making free choices for ourselves. If our emotional programming has pointed us in one direction, perhaps addiction, imagine how difficult it is to break the set of those generational patterns. However, you are actively trying to change by reading this book and working on yourself. This book encourages change to such patterns. With commitment and courage you are helping to put an end to generational shame and addictions, leaving your children freer to make healthy choices in their lives as they will witness your own healthier choices. The Love Addict, in common with other addicts, has learned emotional responses from the parental figures, through generations of trauma, shame and secrets. That is what I learned from my parental figures and it took me into an extremely destructive relationship.

Non-verbal anger

I once had a client being treated for codependence and Love Avoidance, who was ending a relationship with her love-addicted partner. After they had separated she found it difficult to cut the ties and have no contact. She wanted to keep him comfortable, as it was she that had left the relationship. She was carrying the toxic, generational shame of her parents in not showing her anger towards her partner for the controlling and manipulative behaviours he had displayed during their relationship. In her own family it was not acceptable to show anger and it was never expressed in a safe and appropriate way. It was almost impossible for this client to be angry. Her body permitted her to show her anger only in facial expressions. She had also learned to block her feelings by frequently placing her hand over her mouth and by stopping breathing. As a child she had watched her father's face, as it would contort with frustration. Her mother's body would shake with anger, although that anger was never expressed verbally. She had learned to express her feelings through her body; it was the most reliable method of acknowledging what her feelings were. This client was unable to make healthy choices in expressing herself, as she had not been shown how to by her parents. She had emotionally left the relationship a year before coming for therapy, although she had remained with her partner.

She presented with relationship problems. Her body's response to her relationship problems was to withdraw from the sexual relationship with her partner. This way she could demonstrate her only sense of power, as she could not express her anger. The relationship broke down. Her partner had been in deep emotional pain about the split. As she worked on her awareness of her codependence in this situation, she recalled in one session how her last meeting went with her ex. She entered the room, tears began to fall and, silently, she struggled to breathe. Breathing shallowly and not thinking straight are signs of emotional trauma. Eventually, as I reminded her to breathe, she began to relay the details of her meeting with him. She said that her ex had tried to be controlling throughout the evening. Towards the end of the evening he came up close to her face and told her that he would like to take a knife and slowly cut her throat, watch her fall to the ground and laugh as life left her for dead. My client was traumatised by the thoughts of her ex-partner's fantasy. He was emotionally damaged and had threatened her life. How can we know if another person is willing to turn fantasy into action? Had she had taken care of her own needs by observing boundaries, remaining apart from him, and had she not put his emotional pain of her leaving their relationship before her own needs, she would have avoided this serious threat to her safety.

My client worked through the emotional pain of her experience and put preparations in place to keep herself safe from her ex-partner. She found her feelings of anger and was able to process the experience appropriately. Trauma will typically reveal issues of shame and anger along with a deep sense of emotional pain and loss. When we have been emotionally affected by trauma, something inside fragments. Part of us, emotionally, dies or lies immobilised; some people experience powerlessness over a situation that may be driving anger and rage deep within us. In effect, we suffer a loss of self. For those of us who suffer from relationship issues, expressing anger – as well as other emotions – appropriately is very important. Buried anger can feel frightening, and it is common for people to report that they are afraid of their own anger. Others deny having anger feelings at all. A repressed anger needs to be released in a careful and managed way. It may be that anger was not permitted in the family or home environment. Perhaps one or another of the adults expressed anger too freely, leaving others little choice but to conceal their own. Ask for professional help if necessary.

Emotional blocking

Some people may cope with trauma experiences by blocking, blocking the pain by burying it or by ignoring it, perhaps pretending that it didn't happen. This is known as denial. The objective is to protect oneself from the traumatic experience. This may be a child's way of saving him or herself from unacceptable reality or an abnormal event. This type of trauma response may remain a block to emotions that can have negative effects in adult life. Ultimately, blocking removes our sense of reality and therefore separates us from the truth. It shifts the balance from protection to destruction as it moves from a childhood coping skill to an inappropriate coping skill in adulthood.

The trauma that I experienced with my first husband had a profound effect on me. After our divorce he stalked me for two years and on one occasion I saw him take what looked like a shotgun from the trunk of his car. The fear caused by this situation finally led me to have a restraining order served on him. It took me a great deal of courage to do this because he had previously attempted suicide and I felt responsible for his emotional pain. I felt guilty that my ex-husband did not feel happy: he was angry and disapproved of my decision to end the marriage. His feelings were hard for me to accept.

As a child I had learned to feel responsible for the emotional happiness of my mother, and I had also tried relentlessly to gain my father's approval. The pattern had been set for my future relationships, which, in essence, was to take responsibility for other people's happiness and well-being. Reality, therapy, reflection and recovery tell me that clearly I am not responsible for anyone else's emotions or actions. The moment of enlightenment is a powerful experience; it holds the potential to change a lifetime's integrated belief. Thoughtful and careful exploration of family patterns, using therapy as a tool, was the key to my enlightenment. My diminished sense of self led me to abandon self care. Subsequently, blocking the trauma led me to procrastinate over urgent and important legal affairs with my second husband for the provision of and protection, as I saw it, of my two sons. This is a clear example of why it is necessary for us to stay grounded in reality and live our lives in the present.

Unfinished business

It was due to my trauma blocking and use of denial that I had procrastinated. My sons have witnessed this behaviour pattern and seem to have taken on some of the information as their inherited generational shame. It has been a legacy of unfinished business. I have seen this manifest itself in my eldest son's relationship with his girlfriend. He has shown signs of Love Avoidance. His early enmeshment with me has naturally led him to seek needy women. He takes the knight in shining armour role. Blocking showed itself by his being unable to address his own needs within his relationship and attain balance. He was unable clearly and firmly to state his need to leave the relationship. He was unable to be honest about his feelings of emotional suffocation. He stayed in the relationship with increasing feelings of guilt, based on wanting to take care of his girl-friend's emotional needs. Eventually, through a build up of resentment because of his caretaking role, he was unfaithful. (See Chapter 13: *The Love Avoidant personality.*)

As I grow stronger in recovery, my sons will have a better chance of living their lives without repeating the patterns inherited by me. As I grow and learn, I will endeavour to pass on healthy examples to my sons so they may reduce the chance of replaying the agony of addiction. **It is never too late.**

Procrastination may also be a sign of unexpressed anger, as it was in this case. Exercises to release anger energy can be found at the end of Chapter 3: *The balance of emotional energy.*

Trauma bonding, and trauma re-enactment, are the elements within Love Addiction that are most likely to start love relationships with others, in the hope of relieving the original issue, be it abandonment, rejection or feeling unaccepted by the parental figure. This is often played out in adult relationships, giving us an opportunity to resolve the pain. Unfortunately, the choices we make in our love partners are set up from the beginning to let us down, because the choice we make in the first place is stimulated by those feelings we experienced in childhood. For example, we learn to look for the signs of affection that we did receive when younger, maybe the look or the smile, the humour or the smell of a person – any memory that conveyed to us that we were acceptable and raised our esteem. The hope is repeated that childhood loss can be replaced by the new relationship; and objectification and fantasy take over while we put maximum energy into the new fix-it relationship.

Memory of trauma

Most people have experienced some level of trauma in their lives; the actual level of trauma and how we store the memory are key when trauma still exists in our life. It is individual to each and every person. I remember reading an article in the *New Scientist* in which Candace Pert, neurophysiologist, showed that memory is stored through our bodies in tissue such as fibroblasts, plasma cells and fat cells. She suggested that repeated movements, such as those that occur in many different sports, alter our connective tissue architecture, which means that we physically learn to respond to the actions, like throwing a ball and catching it. Repetition of behaviour creates memory that becomes integrated at a cellular level and responds accordingly. Just as a child learns the alphabet, and as it learns to build bricks, it can also learn about trauma. For example, a child may have been fed and cuddled and then put into an isolated cot to sleep; he would have learned that his crying as an effort to complain about his isolation did not resolve his distress, as he was not attended to sufficiently. The child may not have been winded properly and consequently have been in pain. The interpretation may be one of abandonment at a time when care is needed, a mild trauma for the baby. If the child learns to interpret the message, due to repetition, mild trauma may develop in the child's psyche. It is not necessarily trauma that a parent or caregiver intends: it is important to remember that it is the interpretation by the child that is the key factor. Trauma, for example, that leads to fear will have a physical effect on our bodies such as sweating, a faster heart rate, and clamming up. When anxiety levels rise, the body responds in different ways – perhaps vision becomes blurred or hearing and speech become impaired – and we can become dysfunctional and, sometimes, numbness may set in.

An acute attack of shame

I had suffered an acute sense of shame at the dinner in London with Charles and his friends that led to heightened anxiety as my fantasy about him was threatened (see Chapter 1: *A case of mistaken identity*). My senses had deserted me at this time of high anxiety. I had trouble seeing and hearing; trying to put words together required all my energy. My thoughts seemed to jump all over the place. This event revived a childhood memory of being caught doing something that violated my value system. My value system had internalised my family's values; these told me to 'be a good girl', 'not to make a spectacle of myself', in other words not to be seen or heard! I was shamed and my body told me so by reacting in this way, in the form of a shame attack. I wanted to explode and confront Charles in front of his friends about his deceit. In doing so, my body could acknowledge that I was going against my value system. I struggled against my anxiety to say my piece. It was, on reflection, one of the more healthy responses I showed, although I didn't think so and it didn't feel like it at the time. My values were out of balance and left me vulnerable. It was appropriate to confront Charles and doing it in front of the very person who had given me the information made it difficult for him to lie further. I had a physical response to my feelings of shame, a shame attack, because I felt insufficiently worthy to stand up for myself. Although, eventually, I did question Charles in front of his friends, it was with great physical discomfort.

It is important to identify how your own shame attacks occur in order to reduce their grip on you. A valuable exercise to help reduce your sense of shame can be found at the end of this chapter.

Low self-esteem

When we look at the trauma issues of the Love Addict, we see that the distortions in thinking lead to the following thought patterns, identified by Pia Mellody in her book, *Facing Love Addiction*, details of which are in the Bibliography.

'I am worthless in relationship to my partner'
'I need to be taken care of because I cannot survive alone'
'If I don't get close enough to my relationship I'll die'

The primary relationship between child and caregiver is integral to adult behaviour in forming emotional relationships. The child that has experienced major rejection or abandonment may be prone to form a fantasy of the ideal parent. The child may also turn herself inside out to fulfil the rejected part of herself by being whatever it takes to win the love she deserves and craves. The child may integrate the belief that if she is truly seen, as herself, she will be rejected or abandoned, as she has clear proof of this from her initial experience. The child's psyche is likely to develop an understanding that she is 'less than' or 'valueless' as she is. So, the child may learn to behave in the manner she thinks the other person wishes, that is, adapting to the other's needs. Skilfully and in fantasy, the child makes believe that the parent, or major caregiver, cares in their own unique way, which then allows her to fulfil her basic love needs. She puts the adult on a pedestal and creates an all-powerful fantasy image. Thus the child can function and survive the traumatic experience of emotional or physical deprivation.

The distorted belief that she is not worthwhile has now been created and the idealised love relationship is all-powerful and is, in effect, the higher power. This distorted message is a powerful set up for future relationships. It also prevents the development of real intimacy. Intimacy can take place only if we are willing to share appropriately who we truly are. The Love Addict thinks she is not worth knowing and will be abandoned if she dares to share her true self.

The trauma of feeling valueless or worthless is a shame-based belief and can, at a later stage, manifest itself in the form of anxiety attacks, panic attacks and shame attacks. These may re-occur in important adult relationships: nightmares, and flash backs may all hold intense memories of such trauma. The belief of worthlessness is reinforced. Chronic trauma operates in much the same way as unresolved grief issues, in which there is continuing low-grade emotional pain.

Reducing shame

We store traumatic experiences in our bodies in order to access the body's messaging system and through that system we change how we cope with the trauma (Pert, 1999, page 147), both in body and in mind. Massage and exercise can be good ways in which to shift emotional baggage or blockages from our bodies.

The purpose of reducing shame is to separate the overwhelming feelings of shame, which can render us helpless and physically out of control from the true self. As we begin to expose the shame demon, its power over us will be reduced. This is done by gradually recognising the shame, identifying it and separating it from ourselves. We adopt a more knowledgeable and welcoming stance and that reduces the fear and the control exerted by shame. Actively working at separating the shame demon when it occurs is very important as it helps us to identify what is our true self and what is shame.

It may be advisable to take the following exercise to your therapist or do it with someone who is supportive of you. At the first sign of difficulty, which can be identified by a change in your breathing, stop and only re-attempt it with a professional qualified therapist. If you do notice a change in your breathing, affirmations are essential together with a shift in focus to the breathing for relaxation technique.

- ♥ We can use an internal dialogue that says 'Hello, I know what you are, I know where you came from and what you are trying to do to me'. This will help enable you to shift the relationship you have with shame. It may seem simple but, with high levels of anxiety, it can be a struggle. This process may need to be repeated several times in order for you to regain a level of ease. Repeat as often as required.
- ♥ Get to know the details of your shame core, for this is a vital part of arresting the intensity and fear of what will happen if the shame takes you over. It is a necessary part of taming shame.
- ♥ Remember a time when you noticed your body becoming uncomfortable or unmanageable in relation to any significant memory, such as sadness, isolation, fear or threat.
- ♥ Close your eyes and try to put some details into the picture: What were you wearing? What was your hair like? Where were you, do you remember the surroundings? Was there a particular smell present?

What was the weather like? Who was with you? And what were you doing?

♥ When you think that you have enough information, concentrate on your bodily sensations: Was there a tightness in your stomach? Were you aware of a tight feeling in your chest? Did your head ache? Did you take yourself off into another world? Were you sweating? Was your sight or vision impaired? Did you need the lavatory? Did you feel like vomiting?

♥ If you are unable to use your visual senses, and some of us cannot, do not be discouraged. Keep going; more and more information may slowly be revealed. Imagine a colour that expresses your inner feelings. Perhaps this colour represents the trauma. Imagine where it is in your body. Describe what it feels like... perhaps heavy and sticky mud, or fire, or blood. Put an image to it, perhaps a ball or something sharp, or perhaps it runs through your veins like a cold, black river?

♥ Write down on a piece of paper when this shame feeling first began in your life. Who was the perpetrator of the shame? Do not worry about betraying the other person; you can concern yourself with other people's feelings when you have become the master of your own.

♥ What are the triggers for your shame? For example, which times or events are most likely to bring on a shame attack? Use this knowledge and flag it up for yourself in future. What has been the result of the shame? For example, did it keep you back in life, and was it limiting your potential? Did it isolate you? Has it kept you from being sexual or made you too sexual? Has it kept you from pursuing your preferred career? Has your sense of shame stopped you from marrying, having a family or travelling?

♥ Now write a letter to the perpetrator, handing back his/her shame. Explain that the shame does not belong to you and that you have no further need for it in your life. Tell the shame that you know where it came from and that you know what its job has been. Explain that it is now fired, sacked, from your life. This critical and judgmental part of your inner world is no longer needed.

Two very important techniques to relieve anxiety are: (1) breathing, taking deep belly breaths as described in greater detail in Chapter 7: *Healthy breathing*; and (2) affirmations, which should be said like a chant, over and over again, until the anxiety passes. (See Chapter 8: *Affirming your self and your beliefs*.)

Congratulations, now you are on the way to reducing your shame.

KEY POINTS

- ❤ Shame can overwhelm your life
- ❤ Teach yourself to let go of inherited baggage
- ❤ Expose the shame demons
- ❤ Toxic shame is carried through the generations
- ❤ Toxic shame holds you hostage to achieving your true potential
- ❤ Sex can be mistaken for love
- ❤ Release the shame and find yourself.

Chapter
6

Self-esteem – learning to value yourself

The core elements of self-esteem are boundaries, reality, dependency, moderation and balance: and these are integral to recovery from Love Addiction. Without working on these issues in relation to ourselves, the pattern of disastrous and painful relationships is likely to continue.

We all possess self-esteem: the important question is to what degree or measure do we have it? Self-esteem is the internalised, inherent value we have of our self, our own approval and acceptance of who we are as a person – our individual identity. Too little self-esteem can affect our behaviours and thinking with serious effects, while too much may also prove destructive.

This chapter is concerned with the development and importance of self-esteem: self-esteem that is too high; what is known as 'other' esteem, in which someone gains their sense of value not through his/her self but through achievements and acquisitions such as status, jobs, possessions or through a love partner of a higher status than themselves; and, most commonly, self-esteem that is too low.

Too little, too much or other esteem are all rooted in carried shame, which is underpinned by trauma, as we saw in the previous chapter. Abandonment or distortion of self serves to mask the self that is believed to be defective or even loathsome.

The development of healthy self-esteem

As children we gain our self-esteem by the subtle, yet clear, messages that we receive from significant relationships and influences, affirming our inherent value and worthiness in the world. While each of us deserves a balanced and healthy self-esteem, we may suffer much damage through the distorted messages we receive from our parental figures. Such damage may not be intentional. The damage may be caused by our parents' own low self-esteem: when projected on to another person, it is known as 'carried', as we saw in the previous chapter. This is an important concept as it depicts clearly that this distorted message belongs not to the receiver but to the giver.

Too much self-esteem

The effect of having too much self-esteem (the 'better than' stance), perhaps behaving arrogantly and in a grandiose manner, may send messages of judgment or condemnation towards others. These messages make it unsafe for others to develop intimacy with that person or get to know his or her true self.

A feeling of 'better than' can create grandiosity and arrogance in the sufferer and fault finding with others. 'Better than' is manifested as a feeling of superiority, a false sense of power, and this acts as a wall separating the sufferer from others. This is likely to have originated in a family that has taught the child that s/he is better than others, and instilled a belief in the child that s/he is the family hero or the special child.

Other esteem

Esteem that is derived from what we own or think we own, e.g. children, produces a false sense of power, value or worth. This is not to be confused with a true sense of self. Other esteem reveals itself as a need for important status, a high level job, and successful children; indeed, there are many ways in which the person can measure their value in the world.

One Love Addict client reported that she wanted her knight in shining armour to be dazzled by her and to put her on a pedestal. He would be safe, secure and famous; other people would notice her and she would acquire other esteem. Eventually, she continued, as each partner turned out to be 'real', it was disappointing. Once reality hit with a crash, her sense of self-esteem once again diminished. This shows how a Love Addict searches for esteem. Material possessions cannot be a measure of judging and valuing our selves and neither can our partners lend us self-esteem. Possessions reflect achievement rather than one's own intrinsic merits and personality traits.

Low self-esteem

A feeling of 'less than' comes from shaming experiences involving other individuals who themselves are likely to have self-esteem issues; they may compensate in many ways to disguise their own sense of distorted self-worth. The child is unable to shake off the message of low self-value and integrates the belief of being innately 'less than' or worthless. This can happen, for example, in the family that is compelled to give to others, perhaps through religious beliefs. It is likely that their sense of worth is gauged by how much they help others and are seen to help others in the process ignoring their own needs and wants.

If self-value and self-worth remain dependent on the value and worth given by other people through their opinions and approval, low self-esteem and codependence are likely to come into play. It is the self that learns to be dependent on the approval of others in order to gain a false self-esteem. Take other people's approval away and self-esteem plummets. Codependence is exhausting and, if it becomes such an integral part of managing our low self-esteem we do not regard it as exhausting or damaging. The likelihood is that the progression will end in burn out. Eventually, however, the symptoms become so exaggerated in their intensity that it is difficult to deny the exhaustion. Codependence represents an extreme abandonment of self. (See Chapter 11: *Interdependence within love.*) It is understandable that such extreme pressure of self-abandonment may have physical symptoms.

What goes wrong?

We all have suffered at some stage some type of trauma, whether mild or serious. With all the love in the world, we cannot avoid trauma at some level. Experiences that are sad or frightening or which send messages of rejection can all prove traumatic. These events are often integrated into our life experience. For some, however, the experiences may be more significant and may remain in the subconscious, which is alert, waiting for the replay, poised to recall our original physical responses. The child that suffered rejection and abandonment may take into adult life the trauma memory of those feelings and emotions. The recall may present in the form of anxiety responses, such as sweating or palpitations, at the thought of serious abandonment from the present day partner. The child that suffered physical abuse of one kind or another by an adult may in adulthood fear repetition. The adult parental figure may attempt to gain power and control over the child in order to compensate for her perceived lack of power in other areas of her life, now creating a child that takes the blame for everything that goes wrong. Our bodies store the memories of all our life events that have led us to respond in significant ways (Pert 1999). The more intense the trauma, the more ready the body is to recall the response and protect the psyche – with accompanying emotional damage and loss of self-esteem.

An attitude of either superiority or inferiority may develop in childhood, depending on the message from family members. Thus, a false sense of self is built on a swamp of toxic shame. The child who is vulnerable to the family's belief system internalises the powerful messages they transmit and takes them on as her own.

The child may grow to believe that he or she is better than other people, only to find in the adult world that the family will not always be there to affirm that view. If the family role for the child was that of hero, the message may be integrated as falsely empowering (superiority/ 'better than' stance). Conversely, the family may disempower the child (inferiority/victim stance), through unrealistic and too high expectations. The child may feel overwhelmed and need to escape the family's expectation. Such a series of events may produce the fight or flight response, which may lead either to becoming the victim or the abuser in relationships. The person caught in such untenable situations may elect for isolation as his only option, as that successfully separates him from the unrealistic expectations of others.

A pattern of these situations or positions may develop, as illustrated by the Karpman triangle, formulated in 1968 by Stephen B Karpman. Each emotional role is shown in relation to the other; and each stance may lead to a cycle of behaviour such as victim, perpetrator, and rescuer. Any true sense of self-value and worth is abandoned in the confusion.

Always remember that if a person is willing to rescue you, she is just as likely to move into the martyred victim role at some later stage and equally likely, too, to move into the abusing perpetrator role.

Recognising self-esteem issues

Our body is one of the best tools we have for revealing what is happening to us emotionally. We need to learn that we can rely on its messages and take heed: do not ignore your body's messages. For example, the child who complains of regular stomach aches before school may be trying to show that there is a problem. Parents need to observe such signals and act upon them positively. Ignoring this type of physical message can lead the child to think it has little value or worth. It is offensive to think that any one of us does not have value or worth. We do not need to say or do anything special in order to receive this vital message. When we pay heed to our physical signs this can be an ideal time to address the heavy burden of emotional pain that has been carried around for too long. This is usually a difficult, challenging period, as now our entire belief and value system needs to be adjusted. With support and care from therapists, from medical professionals, from friends and family and perhaps from group support – such as many of the twelve-step support groups – a healthy balance and improved self-esteem can be achieved. Information on support groups can be found at the back of the book.

Our body stores the traumatic information at cellular level within our body's memory system. It lies dormant until external forces that ignite the trauma memory stimulate us. Brain chemistry alters and we respond to the emotional message, accordingly (Pert, 1999). The result is that our inner child, the child within each of us, becomes stuck emotionally at a certain stage of development.

It is perfectly acceptable to reconnect at times with the child within (see Chapter 5: *The burden of shame* (the inner child)). It is essential that we do this at times in order to live an integrated and harmonious life. A piece of music or a particular smell may ignite the playful inner child. The inner child may lead us to dance and recall happy, deeply nostalgic memories. Alternatively, some triggers may occur that connect us to the child within that may be angry or sad at the recollection of trauma.

We have seen in the previous chapters how our family relationships or relationships with our major caregivers, may influence our psychological development. It is the important early stage of development, the beginning of relationships, that is the true foundation of the problem of inappropriate self-esteem. The significant care-giving individuals who were entrusted with our innate value and worth may have influenced the inner sense of self that was integral to the development of our self-esteem, enhancing or decreasing the value of our self. In my experience, caregivers rarely intend to harm; in fact I have seldom come across another human that has intended to do so. We may be inappropriate with our feelings, even explode into rage, but seldom is the objective to cause harm to the child. An exception is those people who have what is now known as 'antisocial personality disorders', formerly called sociopaths and psychopaths.

A child can innocently misinterpret information, but, nevertheless, the message remains powerful within the child's psyche. The father who has gone to war to defend his country, leaving his child at home, exemplifies this: the child interprets, falsely, his absence as abandonment, causing her to feel unworthy of being loved. Another example would be that of the mother who died when her child was young: the child's feelings resemble those of abandonment, although the mother would not have had any power over the outcome, except in cases of suicide. However, the child will experience the real emotional pain of abandonment and his/her self-esteem will likely suffer as a result.

We derive our sense of true value when we are appropriately cared for by parents or people that know how to inculcate self-esteem in a child. Unfortunately, if the parental figure has esteem issues we will take these on; this is known as 'carried esteem'. Both beliefs, 'better than' and 'less than' create dysfunctional states of unreality.

We hold on to our memory at molecular level, releasing messages through our entire body that will respond to the correct chemical information (Pert, 1999), for example, physical signs that let us know when to be on the alert, where there is fear or threat. I recall how I interpreted it when my father's body would vibrate with anger. He would need only to walk past me or into a room and I would be able to detect his anger. It was as if he emitted a message of 'don't mess with me', 'don't challenge me', don't come near me'. I would be ever vigilant and sensitive to his anger or rage; I never knew where or when the line would be drawn between fun and disaster. Consequently, I became very skilled at detecting who was angry.

I remember that I would test the line between fun and disaster by pushing for a response, as a way of discovering where the ever shifting boundary was. I had as a child to develop an understanding of what was safe and what was not: but the success of this exercise depends on the caregiver's consistency. It is difficult to establish reliable information from a caregiver who is inconsistent in his/her feelings and psychological boundaries. (See Chapter 9: *Recognising boundaries in relationships*). Consequently, I grew up without healthy boundaries. Self-esteem may be damaged by not having healthy boundaries as a child, for a child needs to have a reliable way of knowing what is appropriate.

When we have developed a balanced value system, we have a secure environment in which to build boundaries. Unfortunately, with dysfunctional thinking brought about by damaging childhood experiences or damaged family systems, our bodies respond again to the distorted messages. A person with damaged self-esteem, who has internalised the belief that he or she is 'not good enough' or that he or she is 'ugly', will retain the distorted thought that the information is true. The body expresses itself through its physical language – known of course as body language. The body may hold itself in a low or weak position or, alternatively, in a dominant position, depending on our mood at that time. The physical memory that has normalised this repeated behaviour leads the body to believe that the information is correct (Pert, 1999). Therefore, the information that the chemical body waits to respond to is incorrect and far from reality and we must reverse our mental patterning, replacing the old, internalised messages with reality thoughts such as he or she is a 'beautiful child of the universe' or that he or she is 'enough' just as they are. Every baby born into this world is beautiful and worthwhile and 'enough'. Unfortunately, however, it is the negative experiences that occur from birth, through trauma and/or a damaging environment, that disturb this essential truth. (See also Chapter 8: *Affirming your self and your beliefs.*)

A recognisable cycle

We have seen in the previous chapters that one of the early and strong attractions for the Love Addict is the conviction that they have found their knight in shining armour or their superwoman; they are seduced by the other person in the rescuer role. This cycle of behaviours can be played out within any time frame, perhaps over the course of one year, one month, or one day. The cycle may also be played out in any relationship and not only within a love relationship. Become your own observer and see if you can recognise the patterns of behaviours in yourself and in others, too. (If you do this, be mindful not to share your information inappropriately; for example, it may not be in your best or others' interests to share such observations with people who are unaware of your psychological knowledge, so practise discretion.) When a love partner has offended the Love Addict, by, for example, 'acting out' in the addictive process in some way – such as telling lies, working excessively, abusing alcohol or drugs, or hiding behind a wall of separation and anger – the Love Addict will usually retreat hurt and may gather her strength in order to wreak revenge. This is, typically, the point at which the Love Addict either returns to the offending relationship or moves on to search for another abusive and abusing relationship, thus maintaining the destructive cycle and, eventually, an inevitable loss of esteem.

I felt that I had been cheated of revenge as Charles had died; it took me some time to get over the fact that I couldn't kill him first. Of course, I was no threat as a murderer, although such crimes can occur, as I said in my *Introduction*. I could not confront him, I could not question him.

The person suffering from disturbed self-esteem is unable to love and accept himself or herself or another person in a mature and psychologically healthy way. The familiarity of the pattern will lead to further relationships that also replay the distorted message. The individual cannot break away from the familiar pattern, despite the fact that the relationship may be abusive, and here codependency is a factor. Shame and low self-esteem are important factors in codependent dysfunctional behaviours. You can find out more about codependency in Chapter 11: *Interdependence within love*. If the traumatic event occurred at an early child ego stage (early time of development), the survival mechanism almost certainly taught the child to adapt to their unmet psychological needs. Children have learnt to adapt to their emotional environment usually by the time they are aged seven years. A child will attempt many creative ways of making sense of their experiences: this can be when the real damage is done, since it creates a template of learned coping and survival skills.

Denial

Imagine little Emma not understanding why her Daddy does not show his love and affection to her like her friends' fathers do to them. The confusion is easy to empathise with. Emma begins to think that she needs to change herself, so she will become whatever she needs to be if only she can have the love she deserves. Emma dare not show her true self as incoming data tell her that she is not lovable for who she truly is, perhaps leading her unconsciously to think that she is deficient in some way, a powerful shame thought. The child uses denial as a form of protection for her survival. Denial has positive benefits for a child struggling to cope with early experiences. When the child grows into adulthood, and continues to use denial as a protector, there is likely to be excessive vulnerability and a lack of self-protection, both of which cause significant problems.

A key element of Love Addiction is denial and this is one of the hardest obstacles on the Love Addict's road to recovery. Denial acts as a block to reality, separating us from the truth. And, if we are holding on to denial, how can we recognise that? Because denial will itself deny its existence. Separation from denial requires gentle enlightenment because at the core of denial is the desire for protection. Protection by means of involuntary denial may have saved both soul and mind of the Love Addict in the past. It may be that the inner child is still desperately searching for love from the father, mother or other parental figure. The Love Addict may, therefore, through the cycle of relationship repetition or re-enactment, be exposing herself to a series of relationships that from the beginning are destined to reject her, thus still denying the true love that she seeks. This painful compulsion causes chaos throughout the lives of Love Addicts and those close to them. Familiar experiences from the past underpin a series of patterns that can progress to habits, which may progress into compulsions and, eventually, into addictions.

Chemicals in the body strive to make us feel good (Pert, 1999) – and develop a healthy self-esteem – by calming the intensity of emotional distress, anxiety or stress caused by early trauma experiences. The trauma experience may drive us to satisfy the feel-good factor. Love has been compared to an attempt to satisfy a hunger rather similar to eating chocolate in order to achieve satisfaction. It is a physical attempt to experience pleasure. It makes good sense that we humans attempt this strategy in order to feel good. However, it becomes self-defeating when our choices become unmanageable in our excessive attempts to satisfy the craving. Again, the more repetitive the behaviour, the more likely that an addiction forms with an accompanying loss of self-esteem.

Denial, for the Love Addict, because of the early stages of her child-hood emotional development, has become the survival mechanism. Because of her use of denial, involuntarily, she is set up to repeat the trauma of feeling unloved and not worth knowing, even into adult relationships. As a desperate attempt to find the love that was so tragically denied in child-hood, the adult attempts to complete the unfinished cycle of parental love through an adult love relationship and, in this way, regain self-esteem.

A child is naturally born dependent on its caregivers. However, if a trauma happens in the child's early life experience, an emotional block can occur. This may lead to immaturity issues later in life as the develop-ing child progressing into adulthood constantly strives to have depend-ency needs adequately met.

The drive is for relief of the stress caused earlier in the individual's life experience by continuously attempting to satisfy these unmet needs. This block can keep many an addict in a most dissatisfying position of attempting independence through self-medicating their internal stress with addictions. For the Love Addict it is a most dissatisfying cycle as they try to sooth the childhood stress and anxiety of abandonment and loss of value by replacing the parental relationship with a love relationship.

The cycle is itself self-defeating as the adult must first realize that it is impossible to repair the childhood damage whilst in a child state. Independence can be reached only from an adult mindset. It means that a strong sense of self and esteem need to be in place first.

Thinking patterns that are based in unreality can be likened to the anxious inner child driving rather than riding on the bus. Healthy func-tioning requires our inner child as a passenger on board the bus but not in charge or driving it. We need to learn to nurture the anxious inner child and allow ourselves to accept our fears and anxiety in order to move for-ward from an arrested developmental state and develop a truly balanced, healthy, joyful self-esteem.

Raising your self-esteem

Breathing	Teach yourself to remain calm in the face of shame or panic by keeping a regular breathing regime in place. Let this become a second nature practice to help you balance your physiological and emotional needs (see Chapter 7, *Healthy Breathing*).
Affirmations	Develop a committed regime of regular affirmations (see Chapter 8, *Affirmations*).
Exercise	Maintain a gentle regular exercise discipline – no more than 3 or 4 times a week for a period of 40 to 50 minutes as exercise itself can become addictive.
Boundaries	Examine relationships you have that are nurturing to yourself and those that are less so; work on your boundaries in order to restore a nurturing alliance (see Chapter 9, *Recognizing boundaries*).
Separation	Observe situations and how others interact and detach from those who are toxic to you. Literally step back and choose not to engage yourself in self-defeating relationships.
Self care	Commit to nurturing your self and meeting your own needs.
Reality check	Take a reflective view of your life and where you would like to see yourself in the future. Write about your goals for your relationships and your future path. Make a list of steps you can take to put yourself on the road to creating healthier relationships and signposts for the future. Perhaps even consider relocating to another town or retraining for a different career path.

Commit to your self care and observe your self-esteem rise.

KEY POINTS

- ♥ Genuine self-esteem is inherent self value
- ♥ Self-esteem may be diminished or damaged by early dependency needs not being met
- ♥ Arrogance may reveal unrealistic and inappropriately high self-esteem
- ♥ We block reality through denial, a subconscious, involuntary avoidance of truth.

Chapter
7

Healthy Breathing

We need to understand and appreciate the importance of breathing as a powerful tool in the process of our recovery from shame and to witness the effect that breathing has on both body and mind. The Love Addict can combat impulsivity by using controlled breathing in order to slow down the process between thoughts and actions. We need to combine good breathing technique with powerful affirmations in the process of recovery from the shame caused by trauma (see Chapter 5: *The burden of shame*). The importance of affirmations is discussed in the next chapter, Chapter 8: *Affirming your self and your beliefs*.

Preventing health problems

Breathing is a vital mechanism that is fundamental to our recovery of self. If we do not do it correctly, our health may suffer. Not breathing sufficiently may well produce symptoms such as chest pain, raised blood pressure, headache, migraine, stomach pain, or digestive disorders.

Transforming our thinking patterns

By slowing our body and thinking down we are able to create pauses between thought and action. In order to slow down our thinking patterns, so that we may make changes to them, it is important first to slow down our bodies. This is important, as the pauses will give us an opportunity to make changes that should lead to a healthy way of being. Breathing is the first step in this process. When we identify what it is that we would like to do differently, we can slow down and apply the changes.

- Identify what needs to change for you.
- Raise your awareness by observing yourself at these times of stress, anxiety, sadness or anger; slow down and choose to stop yourself; become mindful of what is happening.
- Observe at what times, where and how you think or behave in the way you are choosing to change.
- Use your breathing technique to slow down and to help you retain a physiological and psychological balance.
- You may need to move away from the stressful area or environment to give yourself better support.
- Give yourself between three and six good strong deep breaths and exhale slowly and mindfully whilst filling yourself with positive affirmations.
- Decide what it is you would prefer to think or do differently and use this new way in place of the old thinking or behaviour. It may be useful to imagine taking a step back and disengaging from the emotional charge.
- It will take time to effect a change and you may feel very uncomfortable and perhaps even strange during the process. However, it is a time well spent; you deserve to give yourself the benefit of changing old self-defeating patterns.
- Stick with it!

CHAPTER 7

Reducing stress

Fight or flight is our biological response to anxiety and stress. It is an ancient brain stem mechanism. Our body receives a message from external influences or internal thought patterns that moves it into survival strategy. This biological response will always affect our breathing pattern. The chest uses twelve muscles to bring in half a cup of oxygen whereas the stomach uses one muscle to bring in six cups of oxygen. Some signs of breathing ineffectively are yawning, light headedness, difficulty in catching breath. We may also suffer physical reactions such as dizziness, becoming easily fatigued, headache, clenched jaws, restlessness, raised blood pressure, impaired memory, palpitations, or frequent urination. Some psychological responses include hyper vigilance, difficulty in falling asleep, stress, anxiety, tension and fear. Using good breathing technique can help you overcome some of the conditions listed above, together with others that you may experience yourself.

Breathing for life

Practise breathing as a healthy part of your everyday regime. Take time now to fill in the pauses between your thoughts by replacing the negative comments with affirmations that are kinder, more supportive and more helpful statements. This may feel uncomfortable, particularly if you are not used to this nurturing style of inner comment. Do challenge yourself and commit yourself to repeating the positive messages. It really does work, so persevere.

♥ In order to breathe in the correct way for the purpose of relieving tensions and stresses in your body, you need firstly to find a supportive and comfortable position to be in. This can be anywhere that is comfortable for you. You may prefer to stand, so that your diaphragm is completely unimpeded. Close your eyes if you wish and imagine the happy Buddha ...visualize the full stomach he has.

♥ Breathe in deeply to the stomach using your diaphragm, filling yourself up with as much oxygen as possible and extending your belly to its maximum capacity. You will feel your diaphragm expand. It is not as easy as you might imagine and it may take some practice.

♥ When you have extended your belly and filled your lungs with oxygen, imagine in your mind's eye all your internal organs being enveloped by the fresh and healthy oxygen that now surrounds them. Imagine any stresses or tensions becoming submerged by the inhaled oxygen.

♥ Hold your breath for a second or two, and, now, gently, slowly release the breath. Imagine that you are blowing little feathers into the air and watch them dance in front of you. This should be a controlled action. You should refrain from rushing the process and allow yourself to do it slowly. As you do this, you will receive the benefits of relaxation and soon feel less burdened by tension and stress. Again with your mind's eye, observe the areas of stress being carried away with each breath you exhale.

♥ As you breath out, observe the tensions leave your body, feel the heaviness of your body and appreciate the relaxed state you have created. As a result you will be more present in the moment and more able to take part in what goes on round you, functioning at a level that allows you to balance your thoughts and behaviours.

♥ If you begin to feel light-headed or unwell, stop the process and consult with your doctor. If you notice that you are breathing shallowly or rapidly, make sure that you take time out. Just start breathing normally and take time to explore what it is you are thinking about that may be triggering anxiety.

Develop your breathing techniques

Breathing well is one of the simplest ways to help you recover from stress, anxiety and panic. You can do it unobtrusively and privately, saving any possibility of embarrassment.

Rhythmic gentle sports such as swimming, or cycling, or walking also improve and deepen breathing and calm the mind. Singing teachers and swimming instructors can teach you how to breathe properly and both these activities relieve stress as well.

You may find that meditation and also some relaxation techniques, such as T'ai Ch'i and yoga, are excellent methods of strengthening your breathing, while, at the same time, increasing your ability to create space for inner peace and harmony. Both Love Addicts and Love Avoidants will find these techniques helpful and restorative.

KEY POINTS
- ♥ Become aware of your breathing
- ♥ Modify your breathing to overcome stress and tension
- ♥ Combat impulsivity by observing and controlling your breathing
- ♥ Slow down your breathing in order to calm yourself
- ♥ Use breathing as a tool in the process of change and recovery.

Chapter
8

Affirming Your Self and Your Beliefs

The power of affirming statements need not be doubted. Making affirmations is one of the most reliable and effective ways I know of alleviating the pain of shame. You can use the power of affirmations to reduce the power that shame holds over you. I highly recommend using affirmations as a means of reinforcing positive and nurturing beliefs about yourself.

Why we need affirmations

We need to expose shame for what it is and how it affects us. We need to separate ourselves from entrenched negative, destructive thinking, which has created a pathway in our brains that makes us believe that the negative thoughts reflect truth and reality. This pathway needs, urgently, to be converted into a conduit for positive thoughts, which are based upon actual reality and truth and not generational shame-based beliefs.

Shame may prove to be a barrier to the process of developing supportive affirmations for some people. The internalised negative voice of shame may try to shame you still further while you are actively trying to change the pattern: I have witnessed clients shed tears in sessions as they have read through a list of affirming statements. Affirmations – or kind and gentle thoughts for themselves – were so far removed from their self-perception that they experienced immense difficulty in simply reading through the list. So, be prepared for a deeply entrenched sense of shame that may attempt to prevent the process of change. It is as if shame is disputing its redundancy letter or its final warning of eviction. Shame may try very hard to stop you from developing a strong and well-balanced sense of self.

A child cannot easily confront its parental figure when inconsistency and fear exist. So, the child may adapt to thinking less of itself in order to remain small and out of sight of the perceived threat, that is the adult: in other words, the child has subconsciously to agree with the adult in order to evade the threat and 'fit in' in order to gain approval. Check your thoughts to see if you get an overriding, internal message telling you that you are wrong to try a new way of thinking about yourself; you may experience guilt feelings if you believe that you have violated your values by accusing people near and dear to you of hurtful things. This is a common way of shame trying to stop you attempting to change your old ways of thinking. Be aware of the strength and persistence of shame, which will try hard to prevent you being kind towards yourself.

Building self-esteem

Affirmations are a most powerful way of building self-esteem, related to the chemistry of the body. If we internalise our negative thoughts to such an extent that we automatically think them when we are affected by life's experiences, our body and our mind will believe them in an instant. The molecules that store information and stimulate our emotions will immediately repeat the belief of being inadequate or deficient at some level. 'Emotions are constantly regulating what we experience as reality' (Pert, 1999).

A destructive, learned thinking pattern could be transformed into positive, reality-based affirmation. Most of us can think of times when we have told ourselves, 'I'm so stupid' or 'Look what I've done again', or 'It's my fault'. These are just a few examples of ways in which we internalise negative thoughts about ourselves. We may say 'I should have': the 'should' is a judgmental, condemning inner voice that maintains the habit of thinking less of ourselves. If we continue to live with a mindset that tells us that we 'should' have done something or another, we will remain in a constant state of discomfort and dis-ease. The drive of 'should', a judgmental and critical approach, reinforces a perfectionist system of thinking. Many family systems that I have referred to in this book origi-nate from family beliefs and values. Some family systems encourage per-fectionism to raise esteem and acceptance. In my therapeutic experience and as a human being, toxic shame is hideously painful – in which one is set up for failure and an entrenched feeling of being 'less than' or 'not good enough' – but we can transform our thinking through regular affir-mations.

Starting your affirmations

Actively visualise yourself pushing the old negative messages out and away from your self. Imagine the negative messages being transported from inside to outside and gradually moving away from you. Watch them leave, talk to them, tell them that they have finished their job and they are now redundant. You are finding a more mature and healthy way to live, which is entirely appropriate for you as an adult. I caught myself in my own self-doubting attack of shame when I decided to write about my mother and father for this book. With kind support from my colleague, Kip Flock, I managed to push out the inner judgmental message that told me it was wrong to do so. I often think of the famous passage by Marianne Williamson; I affirmed myself with these words:

... *'You are a child of God, Your playing small doesn't serve this world. There is nothing enlightened about shrinking so that other people won't feel insecure around you. We were born to make manifest the glory of*

God that is within us, It is not just in some; it's in everyone! And as we let our own light shine, we unconsciously give other people permission to do the same. As we are liberated from our own fear, our presence automatically liberates others.'

Transforming your thinking

Here are some wonderful affirmations that are based in reality and represent a powerful way of replacing dysfunctional thinking patterns. You may also wish to write your own affirmations.

I prescribe choosing six affirmations repeated ten times each. Twice a day, once in the morning and once again at night; make your affirmations your first spoken thoughts of the day and your last spoken thoughts of the day and at any time a panic, shame or anxiety attack may happen.

If you suffer from issues of body image and perhaps medicate your emotional pain with comfort eating, I suggest that you write your affirmations in large letters on slips of paper and place them strategically around the areas in which you may need extra support, such as the fridge and your bathroom mirror. Anxiety can lead to alterations in our sight, hearing or speech, and, if this happens, affirmations will help reinforce the constructive and supporting statements for us at the point at which we may be at our most vulnerable.

If speaking with certain people who may telephone you triggers your negative thoughts, place your affirmations around the telephone and, if you find yourself thinking negatively about yourself, affirm yourself by repeatedly reading your affirmations to yourself. Say them, too, as a kind of mantra at any time that you experience negative or painful thoughts about yourself. It is very important to support yourself with positive thoughts, so regularly practise strengthening your under-used or weak nurturing, self-supporting emotional muscle. Even if you don't yet believe what you are saying, the effect will be beneficial and will eventually succeed in transforming your thinking.

The transforming power of affirmations will take time; remember that you are challenging deeply entrenched thinking patterns to change. I remember hearing about a study on false laughter: the test revealed that even if the laughter began in a false way, it took very little time before that laughter turned into authentic laughter. This is what happens in the case for your affirmations, too, so learn to trust in your recovery and gradually replace negativity with positive affirmation.

Choose your affirmations

- ❤ I am perfectly imperfect
- ❤ I am lovable
- ❤ I am not my behaviour
- ❤ I am empowered
- ❤ I am a precious child of the universe
- ❤ I am a fallible human being
- ❤ Everyone has inherent value and worth
- ❤ I choose love instead of resentment today
- ❤ I am kind, careful and sensitive to me
- ❤ I am joy
- ❤ I am enough
- ❤ I deserve happiness and joy
- ❤ I am no longer looking for the right person for me; I am working on becoming the right person for me
- ❤ I can disapprove of my partner's behaviours while accepting his/her preciousness
- ❤ I attract pleasant, kind and loving people into my life and I nurture these relationships
- ❤ I enjoy, value and respect myself
- ❤ I nurture and value honest and natural relationships
- ❤ I am equal to my partner and he/she is equal to me
- ❤ I accept myself and therefore accept others thinking highly of me

- Ending a relationship appropriately frees me to enjoy refreshing new ones
- I ask for what I want and need, letting go of the outcome
- I meet my own needs and wants; I do not expect someone else to meet them for me.

Practise your chosen affirmations daily. The power of affirmations for banishing shame, for conquering Love Addiction and for discovering the reality of your self and your beliefs cannot be doubted.

KEY POINTS

- You can rethink who you are
- I am no longer looking for the right person for me: I am working on becoming the right person for me
- I meet my own needs and wants: I do not expect someone else to meet them for me
- Become who you truly are and affirm yourself with reality
- Regain the power and beauty of your true self by positive affirmations.

Chapter
9

Recognising Boundaries in Relationships

Boundaries are essential in enabling us to protect both ourselves and others from inappropriate thoughts, feelings and behaviours. As we saw in Chapter 1: *A case of mistaken identity*, ignoring boundaries kept me vulnerable so it is essential to recognize boundaries and implement them.

We are normally taught appropriate boundaries throughout our childhood and adolescence. Dysfunctional families rarely use boundaries. You will have seen in Chapter 2: *Reflection ..... and reality*, in the section entitled: *Where was my innervoice?* that it was only much later that I started to ask myself questions about my relationship with Charles and to think about my boundaries or lack of them. I had failed to protect myself and to observe vital boundaries – because the boundaries in my childhood were both inconsistent and incomprehensible, leading me to be unclear about who I was and preventing me having a sufficient understanding of where 'I' ended and the other person began.

Therapeutic work on our boundaries is vital if we are to protect ourselves from others and from pain and abuse. It is also vital to observe boundaries, and contain ourselves, in order to protect others from any pain and abuse that we may inflict. By containing ourselves, we can protect others from thoughts and behaviours that may be misjudged, mistaken, inappropriate at the time or have no base in reality.

Living in reality

Boundaries are an important element of being intimate with another person. They allow us to know the other person's truth without judgment or condemnation and, equally, to share with the other person our own truth without judgment or condemnation. Boundaries allow us to live in reality, be it emotionally, physically, sexually, intellectually or spiritually.

The violation of our boundaries can constitute a gross personal abuse. We can see an example of this with the child that is not believed about an incident she retells and, furthermore, told that she is to blame. One of my clients had been sexually abused by a close family member. The client's family had not wanted to accept the horror of the truth and, in order to protect themselves from that truth, they blamed her and accused her of being mentally ill. This illustrates an abuse of the intellectual boundary.

Working on reality as a part of self-development allows us to gain a good enough sense of knowing for what we are responsible and accountable and for what we are not. It is an important part of maintaining our boundaries. I often say to clients, 'If it doesn't belong to you, don't pick it up'.

Sometimes we may find that we say too much and reveal ourselves all too soon to people that we hardly know. Sometimes we are mortally wounded by accepting another person's reality, simply believing that the other is right, only later to be betrayed by the truth. This is inappropriate behaviour within a love relationship: it illustrates the child within the Love Addict searching to become whatever is needed to secure the prospective partner, who, the Love Addict believes, will mend her broken heart and give her her own – heightened – sense of value. The Love Addict transmits the unspoken message: 'I'll please you any way I can, since if I don't get relationally close enough I'll be abandoned and if I'm abandoned I'll die'.

Listening boundaries

Protect yourself by listening to the other person talking, assess what is said, filter it, check it – and analyse what you hear. Taking on the other person's truth and behaviours, unquestioningly, without analysis, can lead us to doubt our own judgment and trigger us into thinking that we are 'less than' and 'valueless'. These thoughts can trigger a shame attack, and, consequently, we may make dysfunctional responses and leave ourselves psychologically unprotected despite the quiet voice inside telling us otherwise to protect ourselves. We can only hear the loud voice that is our shame voice. Negative messages – like 'I am less than' – keep us from retaining a happy, robust sense of self. Slowing the process of response by using your breathing techniques (Chapter 7) can help you to make considered assessments of what you hear.

Holding on to a strong sense of self and reality by the use of boundaries and affirmations, as we saw in Chapter 7: *Healthy breathing* and Chapter 8: *Affirming your self and your beliefs*, is crucial in overcoming the shame response we may automatically make when a trigger presents itself. This is when the pauses we learned to make between breathing and taking action, and positive affirmations become vitally important.

Affirmations enable us to change the negative biochemistry that we have integrated at a deep, subconscious level. Low self-esteem undermines the truth that all human beings are valuable and precious. Affirmations are fundamental in changing not only the thought patterns that can overwhelm us in a shame attack but also at times when the self is attacked, be it a critical voice from another person or, importantly, one that has been carried from generations past and integrated into the psyche. Most of us have at times criticised ourselves about one thing or another. This is often inappropriate and replays our childhood role, maintaining us in a position of 'less than' or shamed. The sooner you begin actively to amend the misinformation that was installed in your psyche, the sooner you will start to recover and acquire a balanced sense of self and redefine yourself without an unclear boundary. A clearly defined sense of self needs to be a healthy boundaried self.

Remember to slow the process of reacting to what you hear by breathing slowly and in a controlled manner. Concentrate on deep belly breaths and the breathing exercises shown in Chapter 7: *Positive breathing*. When you hear another's truth, take stock; do not automatically accept that the other person is correct. Their reality belongs to them and, so, before you allow it to permeate your psyche, check it out. If it does not agree with your belief let it pass over you.

Imagine now a listening boundary in a tangible, protective form: something that covers you completely but allows you to see out, such as a zipped diving suit (which can be zipped up and unzipped, according to how you judge the reality of what you are hearing); an enormous balloon (in a protective colour – perhaps gold or white – which allows other people's reality to permeate its sides or not as you wish); or a transparent igloo (with a window through which you can see what is coming towards you and you can choose whether or not to allow reality and truth to enter). Visualising a listening boundary in one of these three forms may help you to remember to observe the boundary and thus protect yourself.

Your listening boundary protects you by slowing down what enters your reality: if what you hear seems real, you can allow it in, but, when it does not, you can visualise that information passing you by. If what you hear needs further thought and investigation, visualise it going into a 'thought-pending' tray, consider later and, if necessary, ask for further information in order to help clarify any doubts you may have. Only then can you decide whether or not that information should be admitted to your own reality.

People who use blocks, or denial, as their boundaries will not listen or absorb what is important to others.

Visualising your new life

Visualisation can be a powerful aid to recovery from addiction. We can change the energy behind our thoughts and so promote healing in specific areas of our mind and body. This process takes place in the frontal cortex of our brain, where the choice of what we pay attention to takes place. It can strengthen the energy behind our thoughts, rather like exercising a muscle: the more it is used, the stronger it will become. If we visualise our own healing, we can control the strength and power that weak areas receive. This can, eventually, heal the negative thinking pattern and restore balance. It may be necessary to seek conventional medical advice and care as well, together with your own healing methods, but it is also important to find your own way of healing your mind and body, using the necessary techniques at your disposal. Visualisation and meditation are powerful tools in the recovery of many health problems, including addiction (see Chapter 5: *The burden of shame*).

To help you recover from Love Addiction, I recommend that you use visualisation and breathing techniques together with affirmations in order to make significant changes not only to your self-esteem but also to the burden of generational, carried shame. Meditation is a successful healing technique: by accessing different levels of our consciousness, it can help make significant changes to both mind and body. A Love Addict needs to pay special attention to what enters her realms of reality, as so much of her love relationship world would otherwise depend on fantasy. It is crucial to be vigilant about what you are being told and check the information before you fully commit yourself to the relationship. So, at the beginning of the relationship, take an imaginary check list with you: be both rigorous and discreet in obtaining the information you need. I would like to emphasise the importance of being vigilant and cautious before fully committing yourself.

Analyse what you hear

Part of observing an effective listening boundary means not only listening but also assessing what you hear. You may like to allow yourself a realistic amount of time in which to obtain information and carry out checks such as:

- ❤ Check his/her mobile phone number and does s/he have more than one? If so, why?
- ❤ Make sure you are given a home telephone number, and, if not, try to establish why.

- Check that his/her place of work exists. After a reasonable period of time (say two months, but less if you have reason to be suspicious) suggest you drop by the office and check the reactions to this possible unexpected visit. If the person is legitimate – and has told you the truth – he/she won't mind.
- Create an opportunity to meet the person's family and friends. Look out for discrepancies between what they say and what the person has told you.
- Use internet databases such as www.192.com to check personal details.

Someone observing a healthy listening boundary (the listener) will evaluate the information they hear; if the information matches their reality, then it will be agreed with and taken on board as a 'match'. If what is heard does not agree with the listener's reality, then it will not enter the realms of the listener's truth and a boundary will stop this information from being interpreted as such. If the information the listener receives needs more back up or evidence, then time may be needed to support the information – a sort of 'pending tray' for the listener.

Talking boundaries

In healthy talking boundaries, the language, expression and inflection used will be appropriate, balanced, moderate and clear, so that the receiver is given clear messages and information. Talking boundaries are important; we need to edit what we say to others, bearing in mind the question of whether or not the other person needs the information. I suggest, therefore, that you consider the following:

- Is the information you are sharing appropriate to the person, place, or time?
- Ask yourself if the information is offensive or hurtful?
- Is this an inappropriate time or place to talk about the information you have in mind?

- ♥ Slow the talking process down, using breathing techniques to help you consider your emotions and your responses.
- ♥ Think about what you say before you say it: this can be done only if you slow down the process. Be careful that what you say is not abusive to the other person or demeaning of them.
- ♥ Be appropriate in your expectations and consider whether what you are asking for is reasonable for the other person. It is typical for a Love Addict to feel an entitlement to excessive attention and forget her needs may be overwhelming for her partner.

Remember that the Love Addict/codependent will often overload a prospective partner with too much information too quickly. This can weaken her defence and her self-protection – by allowing her to become too involved too quickly – if she subsequently discovers that this partner is abusive. The partner with whom the Love Addict becomes involved may feel resentful about the degree of caretaking he is doing in the relationship, and he may then use the information that she has offered against her as a way of venting his anger at her.

Building your sense of self means that you need to state your personal reality in appropriate ways: observing the talking boundary is necessary in order for you to project yourself as a valuable person, acknowledging that you are responsible only for the adult that you are and not any other adult. You need to convey that your thoughts and feelings are a matter of your beliefs and value system and that no one can make you feel and act differently. If somebody says something that irritates you or saddens you, your response may have less to do with the other person and rather more to do with your own emotional energy and childhood conditioning. You have the right to your emotions whatever they may be, only remember to gauge when it is appropriate to share your thoughts and feelings with another person.

By observing the talking boundary and filtering information, you will be able to state your reality in a way that is considerate and respectful of the other person's rights and feelings. However, there may be some situations where you will need to refrain from sharing your sense of reality, for example if it is not safe to do so. You could leave the area and start your breathing and self-affirming techniques. If you choose to do this for your own and the other person's protection, make sure that you share this decision with the other person and where it is appropriate suggest that you return at a mutually convenient time. You could say: 'I need to take care of myself by having twenty minutes' time out and then I will return.' It is important to let the other person know that you intend to return and address the issue. You have a right not to be violated by anyone and the right to choose when, where and how someone else speaks to you. If they cross boundaries, you have the right to withdraw. Shouting is self-defeating and not conducive to sharing thoughts and feelings. Someone with no talking boundaries typically says whatever they want at any time with no regard for what is appropriate and for what is offensive. I advise you continuously to check out what is acceptable or unacceptable, what is threatening and what makes you afraid and, put your boundaries in place.

Physical boundaries

We all have a physical comfort zone, a personal space, which we prefer not to be infringed. Be sure, therefore, you have the space that you need.

- ♥ If someone is too close to you or touches you without your consent, you have the right to let them know that you object. Equally, other people have the same rights and you need to be thoughtful, therefore, about their physical boundaries. If you are unsure about the other person's physical boundaries, ask whether or not you are standing too close to them and invading their space, or, if appropriate of course, if they would be willing to give you a hug.
- ♥ It is a violation of the physical boundary to act inappropriately both with another person's body and with their personal effects. Touching someone else's property – such as their mail, wallet, handbag, anything in their home or their car – without their permission constitutes a boundary violation.

♥ Someone with no physical boundaries will typically stand in someone else's comfort zone and touch private property without permission.

♥ Observing healthy physical boundaries allows people to distinguish how close they can be in terms of physical contact and in terms of personal possessions.

Appropriate boundaries are vitally important for the success of all healthy relationships, whether they be love relationships, or relationships with friends, family and colleagues. Good breathing technique and positive affirmations will contribute to your implementation of healthy boundaries. You will benefit greatly by setting your own boundaries, remembering them even in the heady phase of a new love relationship, and by observing, with sensitivity, how other people set and maintain their own boundaries with you. You can use your own observations to analyse the appropriateness of your prospective partner.

KEY POINTS

♥ Recognise boundaries in listening and talking and in physical interaction

♥ Observe boundaries, reinforcing them with breathing and affirming techniques

♥ Use boundaries every day to effect change, to banish shame and to conquer Love Addiction

♥ Boundaries enable relationships to be intimate, trusting and real.

Chapter
10

Reality – Living In Truth

For the Love Addict, reality is a distant truth when she is in a love relationship because of the strong hold exerted upon her by denial and fantasy. She depends on fantasy for the creation of her idealised relationship.

To enable us to live in truth we need to understand the value and true sense of our self. It would have been in childhood that we developed the distorted belief that we are worthless and not valued. Good, sound work on self-esteem needs, therefore, to be continued. Affirmations and boundaries, as we have seen in the previous two chapters, are key to this restructuring process.

Living in reality is an important need for the Love Addict. The Love Addict is driven by the possibility of resolving her heart's biggest wound: that of the parental figure or care giver denying her fundamental needs and rights to feel valuable and worthwhile, and loved and accepted as a human being. The adult that becomes the Love Addict suffered abandonment as a child and that powerful message becomes integrated into the psyche of the future Love Addict.

A shameful death

The childhood emotional trauma of not being shown that she is valuable causes the child deep feelings of shame, together with the shock and dis-belief of abandonment. For a child this leads to a partial shut down or 'emotional death', what I would describe as an emotional loss experience leading to an unacknowledged and misunderstood feeling of grief. In learning to adapt to the message, the child sacrifices the self. Feelings of loss and sadness are common in the adult Love Addict as unresolved grief issues may be present. Shame is likely to persist until the skills and under-standing required to restore appropriate levels of self-esteem and reduce carried, generational shame are put in place. Only then is it possible for someone to take on the inherent value of self that is her right as a human being. Only now can a good, healthy self-esteem start to develop: 'She is enough'.

Shame that is handed to us by the parental figure is known as toxic or carried shame, as I explained in Chapter 5: *The burden of shame*. 'Toxic' is because it has made a painful and destructive imprint on the emotions of the receiver; like all things toxic they will eventually destroy their environment. For the Love Addict it is like an emotional mini-death, a part of the self that no longer functions effectively. Toxic shame underpins dysfunctional relationships for the Love Addict. She will repetitively seek a valuable and powerful partner who will guarantee her sense of esteem and value, enough to be taken care of forever and ensure that she will never be abandoned.

The fantasy ideal

The Love Addict believes that she will not survive if she is alone because she is convinced that her value lies in connection to the other person, the love partner. The continuation of the heartbreak has led her to numerous disappointments in relationships and she will seek out what she thinks are powerful partners who will fulfil her fantasy ideal. The pressure of being idealised will often lead the partner – the commitment phobic person, for example – to maintain a distance within the relationship. The Love Addict may choose a partner – the Love Avoidant – who protects himself from becoming too close or too involved due to the overwheming pressure to care for his Love Addict. It is a set up for failure or stressful repetition. This situation is almost certain to lead to failure of the relationship – in effect, a disastrous and tragic dynamic that has its foundations in the formative childhood years.

The damaging result of the original emotional pain keeps the Love Addict separated from reality by using denial and fantasy to protect herself. She enters relationships under the spell of fantasy, as we saw, vividly, in my own story in Chapter 1: *A case of mistaken identity*. She obsesses and objectifies her partner to fit her ideal love template and becomes entranced by him. The Love Addict is euphoric about her new partner; he is the ideal partner who will save her from the unbearable pain of the truth, which is her childhood experience of being let down, abandoned, convinced her that she is unlovable and not worth knowing.

Denying the truth

Denial, as we have seen in earlier chapters, protects the fantasy that springs from and medicates inherent shame and low self-esteem. For example, a client who came to me with the trauma of childhood sexual abuse was also suffering from codependence and Love Addiction in her adult relationship. Denial by then exerted such a strong hold upon her that she was drawn inexorably, again and again, into abusive relationships. The emotional trauma of being deprived of healthy love was re-enacted by sexual behaviours designed to receive attention. This courageous lady had coped for years trying to hold on to relationships that she thought were 'love'. She had endured a spontaneous abortion (miscarriage) with a partner who was abusive. She had travelled the world in pursuit of love, hypnotised, entranced in her quest. She was in therapy, working together with her partner, to learn healthy relating… but, before this work could be completed, the time bomb exploded. Her Love Avoidant partner could not tolerate any more of the neediness that he perceived in her. This client had become pregnant as a consequence of ignoring contraception: she had used denial as her protection and suffered an ectopic pregnancy. The experience endangered her life and her future prospects of having children. She clearly needed help from her partner in this situation. This was too much for the Love Avoidant, who felt he was suffocating under the pressure of being so acutely needed. He was working on his own issues of codependence and Love Avoidance. The crisis did enable them to review their own roles in the relationship.

For effective recovery from Love Addiction, observing reality is crucial and the Love Addict needs to focus clearly upon this and take care of herself, both physically and mentally.

The example given above shows how denial can be life-threatening if we do not look after ourselves – physically and mentally – and maintain a healthy grip on reality. Denial can, furthermore, be harmful if we allow someone into our lives and give them too much power and control.

Searching for the truth

The Love Addict will typically give over her power and her control to the person she sees as her knight in shining armour. So, if you are in the slightest doubt about what is being said or done by your partner, hold on to reality, and look for the evidence to support the facts you have been offered. Doing this can mean the difference between a safe, happy relationship and a disappointing or disastrous one. The Love Addict needs reality in order to survive and reject any fantasy relationship and the potential for further devastation. By protecting the fantasy the Love Addict will cushion herself within a false relationship and it will be only a question of time before that relationship collapses or the time bomb explodes. Don't worry about what your partner may think or say about your need to check facts, for corroboration: it is entirely appropriate to protect yourself, especially as past experience may have proved to you that so-called facts should be confirmed.

The importance of protecting yourself

We owe it to the self to stay with reality and care for ourselves in order to avoid physical ill health. Each of us is worth it.

Search for the truth of your partner and allow the truth to reveal itself to you. If lies and deception lie ahead, you need to know as soon as possible to enable you to protect yourself from further abuse. As disclosed in my own story, in the first chapter, I was not open, or receptive, to what some would say was obvious. My relationship with Charles was a matter of psychological life or death for me and I chose time after time to continue my denial and maintain the fantasy. The dawning of reality after Charles's death caused not only the emotional shock of the destruction of my fantasy but it was also reflected in my body, mirroring the inner pain of the shame. Pathological, unresolved grief and anger, for all the pain suffered before my relationship with Charles and culminating with his death, eventually manifested itself physically.

It is important that you become the master of your self, explore which qualities seduce you in a prospective partner, and which hooks lead you into a relationship, as you start to become interested in someone. It may be the intellectual stimulation; a sense of fun; the feeling that s/he is in control and everything will be all right with this person in your life; and the conviction that your inner fears and worries are about to be alleviated. The more you understand about yourself, the more aware you will be and the more empowered you will be to see the truth.

Identifying the hooks for you

- Look at your past relationships and explore what are the triggers that draw you in to a relationship?
- What has your role been? Princess, clown, sex goddess? What has your partner's role been? Master, provider, entertainer?

- ♥ Explore in detail what has been happening in your love relationships. Has your role been parental? Or child-like? Has there been an imbalance between your role and that of your partner?
- ♥ Honour your inner child. We all have an inner child and an inner parent, as well as the adult state in which we function:
  - – Explore which aspect of your self has more control at different times. You may find that at times of stress your inner child becomes triggered. Your thinking and behaviour may become irrational and immature. It is important that you try to retain your valuable, precious adult state at these times.
  - – When you are attracted to someone, try to analyse which aspect of your self is being stimulated – is it the child, the adult or the parent? How old do you feel with this prospective partner?
  - – When you become angry or frustrated, which part of your inner self is being stimulated? Is it your inner child? How old are you, emotionally, at this time? When you fall in love how old do you feel and how long does this feeling last?

Moderation, reality and balance

The inner child within the Love Addict holds on to the hurts from the past, and, at certain important times, can take over and control the adult being. Once you are able to identify your weaknesses and preferences – which otherwise provide an open doorway for the so-called knight in shining armour or superwoman simply to stroll through – you are in a position to protect yourself from Love Addiction. Stop! Don't let them come in. It is not necessarily that they are bad people; it is that they are the wrong people for you. Be strongly aware that your weaknesses may lead you down a self-destructive, damaging path. Reality and common sense tell you that you can look after yourself and that you will continue to flourish whether or not you have a partner. The reality, the absolute truth, is that you can relate, happily and healthily, with another person on an equal level without objectifying that person into some kind of supreme power.

Reality requires moderation and common sense; far-fetched, extreme thoughts act against our sense of reality. The belief that another person can be a knight in shining armour or a superwoman displays too loose a grip upon reality. Children cherish ideas of saviours and rescuers: and they get them from fairy tales.

Folk tales, fables and ideals are handed down from generation to generation. With today's fast moving media and technology, children are fed ideals and stories day by day, hour by hour and they seem more and more extreme. These fantasy ideals are being absorbed into our concept of normality. Movies traditionally show the hero and heroine walking into the sunset arm in arm. We are not shown them arguing and discussing such mundane issues as running the home and going to work. If we were to hope for a romantic ideal, we are almost bound, eventually, to fall to reality with a crash. As I have said, trauma that is consequent to love deprivation in childhood may arrest the child's emotional development, and, in adult life, keep her hostage to the emotional need for love that she craved as a child.

So, strive for truth in love. Nothing is more satisfying, beautiful and empowering than the reality of an authentic relationship – a true relationship with your self and a real relationship with your partner.

KEY POINTS

- ♥ Check for evidence to support what you are being told
- ♥ Take your time in deciding if this person is for you
- ♥ Do not get swept away in the seduction of his/her approval and attention for you
- ♥ You can choose to turn him down even if he does appear to be pining for you
- ♥ Believe in your self, your value and your ability to find real love.

Chapter
11

Interdependence Within Love

Interdependence is the healthy and collaborative functioning between two people in a relationship, a state in which the partners interact with equality, neither needing from, or giving to, the other person inappropriately, which could lead to an imbalance of energy within the relationship. In other words, a reasonable status quo exists. Interdependence is the ideal, the goal of a healthy and fulfilling love relationship. In Love Addiction, however, we see marked issues of dependency (childhood needs) and codependency (self-esteem issues), with which this chapter is concerned.

In a healthy interdependent relationship, of course fluctuations happen and this helps us to remember that we are human beings – perfectly imperfect and fallible, just like everyone else. Life events such as illness may cause one or other in the partnership to rely upon the partner more than at other times.

Listen to your body

It is when there is a clear pattern of one partner or the other giving or needing excessively that dependency and/or codependency may become an issue. Within healthy and interdependent couples, such imbalance will be addressed overtly and expediently. If we imagine our energy flow, we can feel when our levels are low and need to recharge; our body is the best way we have of knowing what our emotional needs are.

I often encourage my clients to listen to what their bodies are signalling to them. Sometimes clients tell me they have been unable to carry out an assignment I had set them that was intended as a part of their processing emotional issues. Let go of the stress and be assured that this inability is the body's way of helping you choose your priority at that time. It may be as simple as your subconscious body informing you that the time is not right for you now and you may not, at the moment, be sufficiently prepared to undertake profound emotional work.

It is important to honour and acknowledge our own messaging system. Dreams are another way in which our subconscious mind communicates with us, giving us an opportunity to identify our needs and wants. It may also act as a protector to enable further addictive behaviour and contribute to denial.

What are our dependency needs?

Our basic dependency needs are based on what all children need for healthy development:

- ♥ Food
- ♥ Accommodation
- ♥ Health and medical care
- ♥ Emotional support and nurturing
- ♥ Education
- ♥ Spiritual openness

Love Addiction usually involves codependency: and it is therefore vital, if we are to recover from that addiction, that we understand not only our dependency needs but also codependency.

Ask yourself if you can agree with the following ten statements, in order to help you evaluate your dependency needs and wants:

1 I deal promptly with health problems
2 I include care of my health as part of my regular regime
3 I eat healthy food, at regular times, each day and ensure that I get sufficient vitamins and proteins
4 I spend sufficient time on myself to ensure that my spiritual and creative needs are met
5 I value and nurture my family and friendships, giving myself enough space and time to take care of my own important needs
6 I take sufficient care of my home environment
7 I am careful when entering into new friendships and relationships
8 I am aware of my feelings and express myself appropriately
9 I use my listening, talking and physical boundaries effectively and appropriately in relationships
10 I ask for what I want, when appropriate, and let go of the outcome.

All children are born dependent and clearly a baby will not survive without having his needs met. The baby also has emotional needs and these are vitally important even though his life may not depend on them.

Dependent personality disorder

If basic needs were not met by the parental figure, a child will adapt to survive, although he may subconsciously continue to attempt to have these needs met, in inappropriate ways, for his entire life. This is known as dependent personality disorder. A person suffering from such a disorder will show an excessive neediness and he will have difficulty in making decisions without constant reassurance from others. He will feel uncomfortable when alone and be preoccupied with having to take care of himself. He will struggle to initiate and follow important self-care. His insufficient sense of self is projected, insatiably, by any means possible. He is constantly receptive to being looked after, for he lacks the self-belief that he can take care of himself. His fear of loneliness reinforces the belief that he cannot take care of himself. He will rarely ask for what he wants, let alone what he needs; instead, he expresses his needs through generalised clinging and neediness.

Health issues can become serious if they are not treated and resolved. The fatality rate of heart attack, for example, increases the longer that the symptoms are ignored. If work becomes the chief priority, and personal hygiene and eating are overlooked, this may indicate dependency issues. Our health may suffer, sometimes with fatal consequences: for example, the woman that repeatedly ignores reminders from her family doctor to attend for a cervical smear and then develops cancer.

Escaping reality

Both the codependent and the dependent personality may find that they are on a continuous quest for a state of ecstasy. The drug addict, for example, medicates and escapes his emotional pain not by seeking professional help or support from friends and family, but by using more drugs.

The desire to escape emotional pain by self-medicating can be seen in excessive shopping, excessive drinking, inappropriate sex, excessive work, and by excessive reading among other behaviours – as a means of denying emotional pain. When dependency issues become overwhelming, we are removed from the possibility of intimacy: we are not able to share the truth of who we are with others, as we really do not know who we are. We are too afraid to acknowledge emotional pain and we are unable to change the pattern. It is only when some significant life event occurs that we are compelled to face reality.

I believe that significant events, requiring a life reappraisal, provide a time to rejoice, for now we have the opportunity to change whatever has been negatively affecting or ruling our lives. When we revisit the infantile state of total vulnerability as an adult, we can rebuild our lives and choose how to design a future that is based on firm foundations. At last we can express our wants appropriately without suffering devastating disappointment. We gradually learn to feel secure, knowing that we can meet our own needs. It may be necessary to address and change our style of living in order to effect a complete recovery and move towards developing interdependent, honest and real relationships.

Codependence

Codependence, which is often an integral element of Love Addiction, is a subtle and often unrecognised dis-ease prevalent in society, simply because it is socially acceptable to be accommodating to others.

Codependent behaviour is all about securing the approval and love of others as an adult, in a desperate attempt to win what was so sadly lost in childhood, whatever the cost.

A codependent takes on the role of **enabler** to the addict: she will enable the alcoholic to continue his drinking addiction; she will enable the sex addict to remain addicted to sex by becoming the co-sex addict. The codependent is the ideal partner for those who need to self-medicate their emotional pain because the addict is unable to give the valuable energy required by a loving relationship: his energy is entirely consumed by his addiction. Addicts barely relate at all with the codependent. The codependent, on the other hand, feeds their own insatiable appetite, and need, for making others feel good and, in so doing, wins approval.

My own codependency can be demonstrated by my first marriage at the age of nineteen. In this relationship I had played the Love Avoidant role because I found the relationship overwhelmingly needy of my energy. My boyfriend had proposed to me daily for six months, without fail! Eventually, in a moment of weakness I accepted. And then I had no idea how to tell him that I had changed my mind. I did not want to see him in emotional pain and I therefore sacrificed my happiness for his, in the hope he would be content. I proceeded to marry him, knowing that it was not what I truly wanted. I had blocked out my true feelings in order to protect his. The task then was how to get out of the marriage after I had got into it. One year later I left, and he attempted suicide to try to keep me connected to him and the marriage. I did not return – and that took all my strength and courage.

Codependents will deny enabling anyone, as it disturbs their self-belief that they are very good, kind and caring people: however, denial is an important symptom of the dis-ease. A person suffering from co-dependence needs approval. She is usually the first to offer help and to be depended upon, available to help others and, most importantly, able to help others to feel good.

Determining problems with codependency

Do you find that you:

1   Feel less important than others?
2   Rank other people's needs or wants above your own?
3   Experience discomfort when you feel let down or disappointed about something or someone?
4   Are harshly self-critical?
5   Put yourself under pressure to perform and achieve?
6   Have behaviours that are becoming out of control or lead you towards problems?
7   Find yourself thinking or behaving as though you are better than others?
8   Suffer from anxietiy or stress?
9   Have health problems that could have been avoided had you acted sooner?
10   Suppress your feelings or walk on eggshells around others?
11   Find it difficult to express anger appropriately?
12   Express your feelings inappropriately?
13   Find yourself violating your own sense of values and beliefs?
14   Think in terms of black or white, avoiding the shades of grey?
15   Imagine others are judging you?
16   Are hasty when engaging in new sexual relationships
17   Suffer from depression

All the above are typical signs that codependence may be present and action to work through recovery may be needed. You may not see all the signs above but if you can see some have an impact on your life you may need to take this further. (See the list of Support Groups at the back of the book.)

Codependent people don't know how to help themselves, so they do it through helping other people. Sometimes they feel over burdened, have too much to deal with, and suffer an over developed sense of responsibility.

Is it really your problem?

If you recognise in yourself an over developed sense of responsibility, try to let it go by visualising a slip of paper, which reads 'It's not my problem': when you feel things are getting too much for you, take it out of your imaginary back pocket and read it. This may take practice, as it may feel uncomfortable at first.

Help yourself by considering the main issues of codependency:

The trauma and shame that I experienced in my childhood that led me to believe that I was not valued by my father resulted in my choosing a partner in my later adult life that fulfilled my insatiable appetite for feeling cared for and valued. Charles always seemed to say the right thing at the right time to give me a sense of approval and value. Because of my love sickness, I was out of touch with reality and unable to stay sufficiently grounded to check Charles's claims, as I explained in the first chapter.

Any relationship for me, as a Love Addict, required a high level of acceptance, approval and care. The codependent may often find herself in emotionally draining, exhausting relationships. Codependents need only watch their energy levels, and where their energy is focused, in order to gain valuable insights. However, they will always find a way in which to blame themselves and to hold themselves responsible for their partner's hurt. This behaviour has been learned during their childhood experience.

The child absorbs the pain

Codependence is learned at an early stage of a child's development. It is related to the emotional and practical energies concerned with taking care of others, namely the giving of energy to the parental figure or perhaps to siblings on behalf of a parent. The child quickly learns that the self has less value than that of taking care of others. The more energy invested in others, the less energy that remains for taking care of the self; and thus the self becomes devalued and less important. The message deepens as the child develops into adulthood that he has little value other than to care for others. The codependent has learned by now that to take care of himself is seen as selfish and will therefore neglect his self in favour of caretaking others, thus improving his damaged self-esteem.

As I have mentioned earlier, sex was one of the methods of the exchange of power between my parents. My interpretation was that I was greatly valued by my mother in the enmeshed relationship with her and, at the same time, not valued appropriately by my father. I, unknowingly, was a powerful tool in the battle for control between my parents. I had learned to pick up unspoken messages and I was quick to discern the atmosphere in most situations and environments. I realised that my father had a profound anger about my existence, while my mother was able to regard me as a trophy.

Anger within close relationships

The anger I felt from my father was the most terrifying element of my childhood memory. I would wet my bed for years until the age of about eight. I can remember hiding under the dining room table in shame, hoping to avoid my father's wrath. Bed-wetting is a sign that may indicate psychological trauma in the child: bed-wetting is deeply shameful for a child and, when punished for it, the child becomes even more confused and ashamed.

The codependent is desperate for approval and finds anger directed at her hard to manage. She will take all the blame in order to distract from the pain of disapproval. The codependent will often not know how to express her own anger appropriately, so passive aggression may be the way in which she chooses to expel her anger energy. Passive aggression can be shown in many ways. It can be described as sneaky or hidden anger, such as deliberately leaving a mess about the house in order to provoke feelings in their partner or family rather than acknowledging and confronting their own sense of anger.

As a child I became fearless in seeking ways in which to vent my anger. I continuously craved attention to prove that I was acceptable and lovable. This behaviour grew from seeking attention from my father to seeking attention from others. I recall how once I stood astride a honey-suckle plant and slapped the wasps dead with my bare hands. The more I could kill, the more satisfied I felt. I was angry, alone and intense. But I had become powerful. Risk-taking became a norm for me and with it grew the need for emotional intensity. I had suppressed my anger and found other ways of expressing it. Risk-taking when carried into adulthood can become dangerous, as many addicts may be able to identify or recall.

Codependents are expert at detecting signs of anger. My son Patrick tells me that he can pick up the anger exuded from his father without even being in the same room. This is a good example of hypervigilance on my son's part, observing anger too freely and readily expressed by his father, in my view.

The codependent often regards his or her own anger as unaccept-able. My son Patrick's own expression of anger is causing him some diffi-culty. He may find it such a fearful or unacceptable emotion that he tries to suppress it. By attempting to do so, it builds up and at times he seems to rage for no apparent reason. Consistent therapeutic work on accept-ance of anger and healthy ways of expressing it are the key to taming and bringing balance to this positive emotion.

Anger release exercises – such as those described in Chapter 3: *The balance of emotional energy* in the section entitled 'Expressing anger is healthy' – will help dispel anger held within the body. Although anger is a necessary protective emotion, the codependent finds it very difficult to access and to manage. Codependents believe it to be unacceptable to be angry as that would give people the right to dislike them and that – with its associated risks of not being valued and of being considered worthless – would be unbearable.

While codependents find it difficult to express anger, they may expel anger in passive aggressive ways that include:

- ♥ Habitually being late, constantly delaying other people by an apparent inability to keep appointments and dates
- ♥ Sulking and being moody
- ♥ Refusing to communicate either face to face or by telephone, despite receiving messages
- ♥ Creating a mess around the house and declining to clear it up
- ♥ Not dealing with important paperwork
- ♥ Difficulty around finances.

Passive aggression is disguised anger. It is just as real as overt anger. This is often the way that codependents choose to exert control, control being very important to them. Losing control often signals danger to codependents. They may need to control others in order to keep themselves comfortable about who they are and to maintain a level of safety and predictability within their environment.

Not the person that I thought

Two vital signs of codependence are avoidance and denial, as both the Love Addict and the Love Avoidant seek to protect their false sense of self. Codependent Love Addicts and Love Avoidants may also tend to extreme behaviours, leading to other addictions too: chaos may be the smoke screen used by the addict in order to gain ultimate control and hold on to their chosen addiction, for example, spending too much money, drinking too much, loving too much – all in the cause of self-medicating the emotional pain. (For more about how we use the protective mechanism of denial in Love Addiction, see Chapters 1, 2, 6 and 10).

A striking difference between the Love Addict and the Love Avoidant is that the Love Avoidant believes that love is a duty to take care of the partner, while the Love Addict believes that s/he has an entitlement to be taken care of forever more. She may have exceptional skills in changing like a chameleon in order to be accepted and loved. One of my Love Addict clients said to me during a session, 'I am just discovering that I am not the person I thought I was,' and she began to cry at the enormity of the revelation. This may be a realisation that is tainted with further shame or even anger. As a therapist I regard this as a most positive sign towards reality and maturity.

It is a hugely powerful and disturbing experience to learn that the coping skills that we have used our entire lives (in order to survive and hold on to the beliefs of being a good, acceptable person) are not based on reality. Learning that the whole performance has been an unnecessary drain on our emotional energy and has kept us from enjoying our authentic self is deeply painful. Codependent coping skills have separated us from our true value and worth, although it is true that those skills have helped us to survive the emotional trauma we experienced as a child at a fundamental stage of development.

Codependent people typically have issues with boundaries (see Chapter 9: *Recognising boundaries in relationships*) and self-esteem (see Chapter 6: *Self-esteem – learning to value yourself*), which can lead to extreme thoughts and beliefs as well as extreme behaviours leading to imbalance and chaos. Codependents – because of loss of self – may also suffer from self-care issues (see Chapter 14: *Taking care of yourself*).

When the time comes, when at last we are able to identify ourselves as codependent, we can find the power to change the emotionally exhausting, hopeless and self-defeating patterns that have prevented us, so far, from experiencing life to the full. Now we can learn about and cherish the person that we truly are.

The paradoxes within the dysfunctional relationship

As we have seen, both the Love Addict and the Love Avoidant have devoted exhaustive levels of energy to re-enacting the primary love relationship with powerful figures from childhood.

A number of complex issues and paradoxes may exist within dysfunctional, love-addicted, codependent relationships:

1 The Love Addict places her object of affection on a pedestal, giving him/her the position of a higher power, believing that her time has come to relax, and at last be looked after by her new partner. The Love Avoidant stars in the Love Addict's fantasy, and the Love Addict has not (yet) been abandoned

2 The Love Avoidant will put an excessive amount of energy into securing the relationship. By so doing, he gains self-value and self-worth only to find that the relationship is not giving him what he wants because the Love Addict is accepting his caretaking role but not returning it in the way that he so desperately needed as a child. He may be angry, passive aggressive, depressed or seek relief from his feelings of pressure.

3 The Love Avoidant interprets the Love Addict's behaviour as needy and suffocating. This reflects the Love Avoidant's emotionally confused and overwhelmed state and inability to meet his own needs as an adult.

4 When the Love Addict tries to take care of the Love Avoidant, the Love Avoidant instinctively wants to reject the thought or gesture, as he sees it as a reflection of him not doing a good enough job and fulfilling his duty. The Love Avoidant, as a child, learned to value himself primarily for his caretaking abilities and even if he is angry that he does not feel cared for he is unable to accept his authentic needs.

5 Because the Love Addict suffered abandonment by one of her parental figures, she fears that she will not be accepted for who she is. Her ability to be intimate has been diminished because she

interpreted her perceived abandonment when she was a child to mean that she was neither valuable nor worthwhile. Intimacy is difficult for her as she has lost her sense of self and any power to be herself now carries too high a risk of abandonment. She will become whatever you wish; just don't leave. The dilemma is she can never be known for her true self as she cannot take the risk of being in a relationship as her self.

6 The Love Avoidant's underlying fear is that he will not be taken care of and thus abandoned; hence his desperate efforts to please and take care of his love relationship in an attempt to secure the attention and care of the parental figure.

7 The Love Addict believes that her partner loves her, the proof being that he is doing so many caring and thoughtful things. She happily accepts his kindness without much thought, never suspecting that the Love Avoidant is slowly becoming resentful and angry with the Love Addict for draining his energy levels.

8 The Love Avoidant will be devastated if the Love Addict reacts to his anger by suggesting that she leaves the relationship, for this now highlights his underlying fear, that of abandonment, that perhaps he has not taken adequate care.

9 The Love Addict concludes that the Love Avoidant does not want to continue the relationship, following his unacceptable anger and display of resentment and pain. The Love Addict assumes that this means abandonment or rejection because she is not acceptable as a human being, reinforcing her childhood trauma and shame of being unworthy.

10 The Love Addict desperately wants a love relationship, and she is likely to feel that she has a diminished identity if she is not in one. The paradox here is that the Love Addict is usually capable of high achievement and coping alone, out of a relationship.

11 Because the Love Addict copes well on her own, the Love Avoidant may think that she is perhaps not as needy as he thought, leaving the door open for his re-entrance into the relationship. His feeling of suffocation starts to subside. He may be lured into thinking that he will no longer be taken over by her neediness. This is likely to

relieve the Love Avoidant's fears and he will re-enter the relationship feeling relaxed. He resumes his subconscious pattern of relating and once again his anxiety level rises as he begins to take care of the Love Addict.

12   The Love Addict returns to her subconscious anxious pattern of fantasy love relating and becomes, once again, the needy child. This is familiar to the Love Avoidant, who is inclined to be excessively caring, and he now attempts to soothe the Love Addict, in what the Love Avoidant may interpret as his fundamental role.

As a result of this paradoxical and utterly exhausting, codependent, love-addicted relationship the time bomb will likely explode; it is a consequence of the dramatic swing between the polarities of withdrawal and intensity. Once this has happened the relationship may attempt to regain its former intensity and search for intimacy. The alternative would be to move on to a new relationship and repeat the cycle. Both of these options will most likely progress the damage to the self and still fail to achieve a sound, healthy, balanced, interdependent relationship.

A healthy relationship depends on healthy boundaries, honesty, respect, integrity and an appropriate, reasonable balance of loving energy between the two partners. For this, interdependence between the two is an achievable balance.

KEY POINTS

♥   Learn to let go of codependency – find yourself
♥   Confront your old patterns; work hard to stop them destroying your relationships
♥   Understand the see-saw effect of a dysfunctional relationship
♥   Be vigilant and know your demons before they have you on the floor
♥   Be 'collusive', in a positive sense: the relationship is about the two of you working together.

Chapter
12

Achieving Balance in Your Relationship

Balance and moderation are the primary keys to a healthy, happy relationship with yourself. In this chapter I look, first, at the issues that can damage a relationship, secondly, at how to evaluate your relationship and, thirdly, at how you may initiate recovery from Love Addiction. I show you how to begin to address destabilising issues, protect yourself and achieve a balance within a healthy relationship.

Potentially damaging factors include:
- Trusting too much, trusting too little
- The allure of spontaneity
- The need for intensity in relationships
- Jealousy
- Deceit
- Denial
- Relief through developing secret worlds.

Damaged trust

The Love Addict continues to search for love in the way that she did as a distressed child. Because she was let down by a powerful or parental figure and as a consequence her sense of trust was broken, a tendency to compensate for the lack of a trusting relationship may show itself by trusting too much. This compounded with the neurochemical reaction to the trauma (as mentioned in Chapter 9) of childhood-needs not being met will likely initiate distrust of her own ability to make sound judgments.

The allure of spontaneity

Trauma and shame, as we have seen in earlier chapters, may lead to extreme, uncontrolled thinking and behaviours:

- The desire for intensity within the love relationship – the extreme highs and the extreme lows – may increase as part of the addiction
- People who are trapped in childhood trauma and shame often mistake intensity for spontaneity. However, spontaneity, which helps us experience life with pleasure and zest, is an important ingredient for a fulfilling life
- Inappropriate spontaneity can lead to us being uninhibited, disinhibited, unboundaried, uncontrolled and even offensive with other people.

It is important to learn that moderation represents a balanced viewpoint of life and offers a healthy way forward to living a fulfilling and happy life, with consideration for others.

The agony and the ecstasy

Addictive personalities typically find the middle ground boring. For the Love Addict the need for intensity within love relationships is likely to build and build. This is understandable, considering that their lifestyle has always encompassed the highest highs and the lowest lows. This way of living can eventually make them feel crazy. When they finally reach rock bottom, a point at which they cannot continue the instability and chaos any longer, the need for stability and calm and the desire for self-protection eventually eclipse the crazed, fascinating, thrilling rollercoaster of the extremely intense love relationship. Many addicts admit to believing that they are invincible, indestructible, and can thrive only upon such intensity – signs, again, of immaturity. As they believe that they are invincible, they are all the more disappointed, perhaps totally devastated, when they are compelled to face their fallibility and potential self-destruction. This profound, powerful disappointment simply perpetuates the lack of balance and the intensity of their life experience.

Continuous and profoundly intense highs and lows prevent them from experiencing their feelings in a manageable, balanced way. The Love Addict may regard the middle ground as entirely grey and uninteresting. She has adapted since childhood to block or deny her true feelings. The addiction becomes progressively more aggressive, with the addict's life becoming increasingly quickly out of control, spinning into perpetual chaos in her love relationships.

A sense of loss

Insecure people (those with low self-esteem) may sometimes experience jealousy, which envelops them in a blanket of destructive, intense feelings. This may reflect their deep fear of loss – and of childhood abandonment – and their lack of individual empowerment. Jealousy can be distinguished from envy in that envy is a regard for something and an observation that it would be pleasant to have that thing oneself. While envy reflects a respectful, balanced wanting and not having, jealousy is distinctly uncomfortable, threatening and ultimately often destructive to oneself and others.

Potential for deceit: easy access

It takes time and thought for true love to develop, particularly for a Love Addict in recovery. Today's rapid communication systems include mobile phones, with texting and e-mail, and Internet dating services for a wider choice of instantly available partners. These communication methods, because of their speed, sometimes work against the development of a sound love relationship. Untrustworthy people can easily engage in deception – by using only a mobile phone and email so that specific details that offer security and reality are not given. This can ultimately support deceptive people in acts of relational harm. Love relationships are the most vulnerable in which we engage. When we do not use our listening, talking and physical boundaries sufficiently well (see Chapter 9: *Recognising boundaries in relationships*), we may find ourselves in an untrue or even abusive relationship.

While both texting and e-mail communication tools can be helpful and efficient in rapid social and business networking, and, in the case of mobiles, for personal safety as well, these communication methods can, equally, be used to manipulate people and perpetuate distorted, destructive behaviours.

Privacy and time out are threatened by the use of mobile phones. The needy person can use them to intrude upon us. Text messages are often distracting, diverting our attention from the person or people we are with. The intruder has won our attention. People have been known to deal with very personal, private relationship issues, such as break-ups, and separation and divorce, by e-mail, fax and text, depersonalising what were once close loving relationships.

Texting can facilitate misleading, duplicitous behaviours by others. When I am working with a client on issues of Love Addiction, I am clear about encouraging a limited use of e-mail and text messaging. If the other person is willing and able to be clear about their part in the relationship, they will be prepared to keep things real, and in the moment, by communicating face to face and by telephone conversation.

Evaluating the balanced relationship

I have experienced the pain and devastation of love-addicted relationships for myself and I can truly empathise with the difficulty of looking to the middle ground. However, the gift that middle ground and balance hold is untold richness and stability and an opportunity for interdependence and intimacy that enables maturity and growth towards true potential.

Moderation and balance will never be boring: it is rich, healthy, fertile ground upon which each of us can develop and flourish. While not offering the agony and the ecstasy of extremes in dysfunctional love relationships, this is far outweighed by the satisfaction, pleasure and fulfilment to be enjoyed through stability and reality.

You may like to evaluate your relationship by considering the questions below in order to determine where your strengths and weaknesses lie and how to improve the quality of relating as you work towards achieving a balanced and healthy love relationship.

Rate yourself within the following questions. Use the range of 0–10 to mark the levels of behaviour in your relationship. For example 0 = low grade, mild, not much and 10 = high grade, intense or a lot.

1 How much time do you spend together? ☐
2 Do you deliberately find obstacles to avoid time spent together? ☐
3 Do you think your partner deliberately finds obstacles to avoid time spent together? ☐
4 Do you seek closeness? ☐
5 How much time does it take to resolve problems in your relationship? ☐
6 Do you allow problem areas to continue to build? ☐

7   Does your partner allow problem areas to continue to build? ☐

8   Do you create distance by means of reading; watching television, sport, spending time with other people, drug use, alcohol use, work? ☐

9   Do you think your partner distances using similar means? ☐

10 Do you enjoy your own company together? ☐

11 Do you think you have forgotten how to have fun with your partner? ☐

12 Do you think that your partner has forgotten how to have fun with you? ☐

13 Can you trust that your partner will have your best interests at heart? ☐

14 Do you have your partners best interests at heart? ☐

15 Do you make sure that emotional support in the form of kindness, respect, and consideration are readily available to your partner? ☐

16 Do you think you receive emotional support from your partner? ☐

17 How much time is spent being intimate with each other? ☐

18 Is sex a mutual and respectful act that brings your relationship closer? ☐

19 Do you think that having sex keeps the relationship close? ☐

The scores will give you an indication of which, if any, areas within your relationship need working through. Extreme scores (high or low) may be a sign of a need to act quickly on addressing such issues. Do seek further assistance if you think it necessary. Being aware of an issue is the first step in changing it.

Initiating recovery

At the point of emotional, mental or physical exhaustion we are offered the opportunity to break the destructive cycle of Love Addiction. It is at this point that recovery is most likely to be initiated, offering us the opportunity of rethinking how we define ourselves, who we are and what we are doing, how we approach a love relationship and the ways in which we relate to a partner. The addict may be reluctant, however, to give up long established coping skills and their reluctance, and fear, may be disguised as denial or arrogance.

Once an addict can build up sufficient trust in herself and her ability to make sound judgements, it is more likely that she will take the risk of experiencing her true feelings with appropriate vulnerabilities. Some of my clients who suffer from Love Addiction, when asked to contemplate partners that are not powerful or very successful in some way, offer most interesting and defiant responses: 'I'm not going to choose boring people!' or 'I don't want to change that part of me; it's exciting.' As I have said, I can empathise with the initial difficulty of considering the middle ground; but we are working here – slowly and steadily – towards considerable personal growth, which will lead to realising your true potential, and towards achieving a genuine richness in a loving and nurturing relationship.

Protecting yourself

Slowing down

We need to learn how to balance and moderate our thoughts and behaviours in a way that is not offensive or abusive to other people. We do not need to be controlling or to be out of control in order to enjoy spontaneity. To think before acting is the best way of slowing down the process of change. Breathing exercises (see Chapter 7: *Healthy breathing*) are one of the best ways in which to slow down body and mind, thus enabling you to consider your behaviours and give thoughtful, mature responses. You will become receptive to replacing dysfunctional responses and behaviours with ones that are more balanced and healthier choices. As you slow down, you will be able to make this empowering and healthy change for yourself. Combine this slowing technique together with your affirmations and your boundary work (see Chapter 8: *Affirming your self and your beliefs* and Chapter 9: *Recognising boundaries in relationships*).

Use your boundaries

Give yourself permission to *use* all of your boundaries even when it doesn't feel comfortable: now is the time to challenge your long established behaviours.

Remember always that it was your former thinking and behaviours that led to love relationships proving to be destructive.

Filter what you say

Be prepared to contain and filter what you disclose about yourself: for example, do not divulge sensitive personal information during the first few meetings or announce that you have just received a financial windfall or inheritance. I am not suggesting that you hide who you are or deceive the other person. For someone who has not used boundaries in the past, it may feel awkward at first putting them into use. The need to feel comfortable and slip back into old patterns often arises. Do resist doing so.

Containment and filtering, monitoring what you say and do, is a mature and reflective way of maintaining balance and moderation. It is especially important for the Love Addict to use the talking boundary when engaging in a new relationship. Refrain from telling your new acquaintance that you love them until you have covered some of the bases that will give you secure information about their identity, such as: what their family is like; who their friends are; where they work; where they live; what their interests are; what their hobbies are and, most important, what their habits and lifestyle are. Can you verify any of this? Simply, hold back for a while until you are sure this person is genuine.

Consider your health

Your emotional, mental and physical health should be your one most important priority at all times. See Chapter 14: *Taking care of yourself.*

Therapies such as T'ai Chi and yoga are well-respected techniques in the pursuit of a balanced lifestyle and well-being. You may benefit by integrating one of these therapies, in thought and in deed, into your new way of living. With daily practice, you will soon no longer need to give conscious thought to a slower, more balanced way of living, as you will develop the techniques for healthy functioning at a subconscious level.

Be truthful

Finally, the essential features of a good relationship, in my view, are integrity and truth upon a solid base of reality (see Chapter 10: *Reality – living in truth*) and recognition of the need for mutual respect and inter-dependence (see Chapter 11: *Interdependence within love*).

KEY POINTS

- ❤ Constantly evaluate your relationship
- ❤ Be vigilant and mindful of your choices
- ❤ Raise your self-awareness and your patterns of thinking and behaviour
- ❤ Slow down – using your breathing, your affirmations and your boundaries
- ❤ Embrace the middle ground: this is where happiness in love is found
- ❤ Keep yourself protected.

Chapter
13

The Love Avoidant
Personality

The Love Addict will tend to find herself drawn to relationships with the Love Avoidant or commitment phobic personality. These two, pretty much indistinguishable types are the perfect (albeit dysfunctional) complement to the Love Addict. You will have seen in the previous chapters how to empower yourself to move away from these personality types, with or without professional help.

I described the complex issues and paradoxes within codependent relationships in Chapter 11: *Interdependence within love*, and now I offer a brief outline of the chief features of the unceasing relationship cycle from which both the Love Avoidant and the Love Addict suffer – and which they themselves perpetuate.

❤ The similarities between the Love Avoidant and the commitment phobe include the speed and intensity with which they start a new love relationship. (For the purposes of this chapter we shall use the term Love Avoidant to describe both conditions.) Seduction will be extreme, flattering and dedicated, with all the romantic flourishes of flowers and text messages: big signals to the Love Addict that she is a very valuable, very desirable, and much loved.

- The Love Avoidant withdraws rapidly from the relationship once he perceives anxieties that are, to him, overwhelming and fearful.

- The Love Avoidant enters a relationship as caretaker, and imagines the new relationship to be everything he ever dreamt of.

- The Love Avoidant may experience great anxiety and a feeling of suffocation when the relationship appears to become too close, resembling the enmeshment he suffered as a child. He may fear that he is devoting an excessive amount of caretaking and energy to the love relationship, just as he once did – and now he worries that it is going to take him over. This is a real stress reaction, a phobia or anxiety response (see the physical signs of anxiety below).

- The Love Avoidant may experience more and more stress and anxiety as the energy required to satisfy the (insatiable) Love Addict increases. Physical signs of anxiety may include breathing difficulties, tightness around the chest, headache and migraine, digestive problems, nausea, lightheadedness, excessive sweating and avoidance, distancing or addiction.

- Underlying the Love Avoidant's feelings of pressure and suffocation are fears of rejection and of intimacy, and self-esteem issues. Usually, the Love Avoidant will have invested a great deal of care and hard work to ensure that he is not rejected and to guarantee his acceptability and approval.

- The Love Avoidant may attempt to hide behind his relationship with the Love Addict, using it as proof of his own value. There may be a tendency to avoid new activities for fear of feeling shame and being seen as incapable.

- The Love Avoidant may create a secret world in which to hide and thus conceal his sense of shame and worthlessness. It is a sad, lonely and destructive emotional state to inhabit.

- The Love Addict may at first believe that she can depend on the Love Avoidant for all her needs, concerns and worries, for until a certain point this is his constant message to her. She is his queen, and he will always adore her. The Love Addict may feel entitled to this elevated status. It is likely to turn out, however, that she is greatly mistaken.

♥ The Love Avoidant may become brusque and resentful of the slightest request for help once he has reached the end of his tether, and anxiety and suffocation take over due to the build up of his resentment from his role.

♥ The Love Avoidant's tether may seem to be very short to the Love Addict, but the anxiety felt by the Love Avoidant produces overwhelming feelings of resentment, anger and fear and the ultimate need to create distance.

Come close and leave me alone

The pressure and suffocation experienced in the adult love relationship reflects the way in which the Love Avoidant related to his parental figure, in which endless caretaking and energy were invested, and yet were probably not adequately acknowledged. Love and attention may not have been returned sufficiently or appropriately. The adult Love Avoidant is the child that was enmeshed with his parental figure, the child who has to relate not as a child but rather as a friend, sometimes occupying the emotional vacuum created by the departed or unavailable spouse. This is a position, created by the parental figure, which entirely lacks the appropriate listening, talking and physical boundaries in the relationship with the child.

The Love Avoidant's unconscious command is 'come close and leave me alone' in order to relieve pressure so that he can breathe freely once again and avoid being overwhelmed by caretaking duties. This subconscious drive is confusing for the Love Avoidant, as he fears abandonment, rejection and ultimately intimacy, on the one hand, but he needs, on the other hand, to recover and win acceptance and approval by caretaking.

The Love Avoidant and the Love Addict suffer similar underlying fears of rejection, abandonment and intimacy. The Love Addict primarily fears abandonment, the Love Avoidant primarily fears intimacy.

'Come close and leave me alone' is a very confusing message for the Love Addict and one that is almost impossible with which to comply, despite her attempts to be everything that is needed, and desired, by the Love Avoidant. The Love Addict is usually a mistress of becoming whatever is wanted, a chameleon personality, in her desperate quest for the love she lost as a child. This consequently leads her into relationships that may be based on complete fantasy, both concerning who she is and also who her partner is.

Fleeing from intensity

More often than not the Love Avoidant's high level of anxiety is likely to cause him to distance himself from the intensity of the relationship in some way. This may be through, for example, excessive work, extra-relational affairs, drug misuse, excessive alcohol, or extravagant spending or gambling – any way in which he may achieve relief.

As in my son, Joseph's case, which I described in Chapter 5: *The burden of shame*, the anxiety that he experienced within his love relationship of too much pressure and suffocation led him to act out. (Acting out describes someone remaining active in his or her addictive behaviour in an attempt to calm and soothe the stress.) He had started a secret relationship outside the one he was already having. It was important for him, as the Love Avoidant, because he needed relief from the intensity of his original relationship. When his girlfriend found out, Joseph's feelings of shame were acute and overwhelming. He was desperate for approval and acceptance and had in fact betrayed his own value system. The consequence of this was his telling me he wanted to end it all. I immediately flew him out to stay with me, where I could explain the cycle of Love Addiction and Love Avoidance. I was able to reassure him that he was carrying family shame and that, although he might have done bad things, he was not a bad person. His self-esteem had been damaged during his childhood and it was now in need of strengthening.

The Love Avoidant may return to the original relationship, once the pressure is relieved, or move on to a new relationship and perhaps repeat the same cycle. The cycle of frustrations, owing to both the Love Avoidant and the Love Addict experiencing the break-up of their fantasy love relationship, is just as real and painful for each partner.

Love Avoidants fear committing themselves to almost anything for fear of (a) not making the right decision, (b) a relationship leading to intense pressure, and (c) perhaps missing out on, something better that might come along. This thinking can lead to withdrawal behaviours and situations, in which the Love Avoidant's partner is compelled to relinquish the relationship, and the Love Avoidant can then blame his partner for her departure when, in fact, it is he who has left the relationship. He may nevertheless claim that it is all the other person's fault: that she was too short, too old, too fat, too unintelligent, or not of an acceptable status, for example.

Fear of commitment can be just as stressful for the Love Avoidant as for the love-addicted partner. The Love Avoidant, or commitment phobe, will often suffer overwhelming feelings of guilt when withdrawing from the relationship and, consequently, may feel compelled to return. This leads inexorably to further repetitions in the cycle of dysfunctional feelings – of being used by the love partner, for example. These feelings reflect distorted beliefs and emotions not based in reality, but on the emotional pain that originated in the childhood love relationship with the parental figure. These feelings may become displaced on to adult love relationships.

Too far, too fast

I met up with a blind date, who turned out to be young, attractive, successful and very intellectual. Now intellect is my personal hook: it is extremely attractive to me and it is a sign that warns me I may be drawn into an addictive relationship. We met on about five occasions; all the communication between these meetings was by messaging service on the mobile and by telephone.

One evening he invited me to have dinner with him at his home. I accepted and we spent a wonderful evening intensely discussing cosmology. We seemed to get on together very well indeed. Afterwards, we shared some fantasies about how our new relationship might develop.

The following weekend, after a couple of intimate mobile phone messages from him, I heard nothing at all from him: complete utter shutdown. His withdrawal was his only way of protecting himself from intimacy and from pressure, as he perceived it. I found this rejection heartbreaking, as I truly believed that we were a great match for each other. Having studied in depth the responses made by Love Avoidants, and by Love Addicts, I now understand that he was playing a part in a cycle of dysfunctional behaviours – and so was I.

No one's perfect

Many anxieties are underpinned by childhood trauma and may be revealed by the Love Avoidant in adult life when triggered by comparable situations. Commitment phobes will frequently find the perfect partner only later to decide, as I mentioned earlier, that their apparently perfect partner doesn't have the right colour hair, is a little bit overweight or is not intelligent enough. The Love Avoidant will always find a perfectly legitimate (to them) reason for not being available in a relationship. He will claim that every relationship misses that essential something so that he does not have to make the fearful decision of commitment. This experience from the Love Addict perspective can cause deep resentment as years may have been lost to their relationship.

I have a friend that finds it difficult even to commit to a dinner date: it is just not possible for him to make any definite commitment. I watch him miss one possibility after another with women and, when he finally accepts an opportunity, he finds excuses to convince himself that it is not the right decision. Sadly, this is a self-perpetuating cycle of disappointment and dissatisfaction, which is founded upon the real anxiety of making a commitment. Depression and isolation become increasingly more evident as a result.

Evaluating Love Avoidance

Answer the following questions in order to evaluate how you relate to others and to determine whether or not you have issues that would benefit from professional counselling or therapy. Use the scale of 0–10, 10 being the greatest degree of the problem and 0 being not much of a problem at all. The scale will help you identify the level of intensity for your particular issues. I suggest that any issue that rates above the scale of 5 may need attention and, perhaps, therapy. Be honest with yourself.

1 Do you have a history of relationships that run into difficulties at the point of commitment?
2 Do you avoid social relationships?
3 Is it important for you to feel accepted by others?
4 Do you struggle to relate to others if it is not a potentially intense or romantic relationship?
5 Do you suspect others of talking about you behind your back?
6 Have you been told by those in close relationships with you that you are cold and distant?
7 Have you been accused of being cruel?
8 Are you ever told that you are moody?
9 Do you suppress your anger?
10 Do you ever rage?
11 Are you – or members of your family of origin – perfectionists?
12 Do you fear rejection?
13 Do you suffer low self-esteem?
14 Do you feel superior to others?
15 Are you critical of others?
16 Do you look forward to a committed relationship?
17 Are you critical of yourself?

18 Are you withdrawn in social situations?
19 Do you fear separation from those you love?
20 Are you considered stubborn or rigid?
21 Have you been described as arrogant or grandiose?
22 Have you ever created a secret world in which to relieve your feelings of pressure?
23 Do you tell lies or mislead to protect yourself?
24 Do you ever feel unappreciated for your efforts?

There are no correct answers to these questions; they are intended to help you focus upon issues of Love Avoidance and commitment phobia. If you think that you would benefit from support with working through some of the issues, contact a qualified therapist or counsellor. If, on the other hand, as a Love Addict, you can identify certain issues of Love Avoidance in your partner, you may wish to consider joint counselling.

It is very, very sad for the Love Avoidant to miss out on the chance of love, and a truly fulfilling loving relationship, just because of unresolved issues and childhood emotional pain. If you yourself recognise the issues highlighted in this chapter, let me suggest that you take the necessary steps to resolve your pain and consider becoming receptive to the riches that a real relationship can offer.

KEY POINTS

- ♥ Enmeshment is inappropriate and damaging to relationships
- ♥ Taking care of someone does not equal love
- ♥ Intensity is destructive
- ♥ Secrets do not relieve pressure
- ♥ Striving for the perfect relationship is self-defeating
- ♥ Keep communication open and collusive within your relationship.

Chapter
14

Taking Care of Yourself

You are important and your physical, mental and emotional health must be one of your first priorities. This concluding chapter is concerned with promoting a stronger sense of self and strengthening your relationships in the future. You can transform your daily way of life by learning to observe your thinking and behaviours, and by using boundaries.

This final chapter looks at:

♥ Beyond Love Addiction – learning new, healthy ways in which to love
♥ Intimacy without addiction – true sharing with your partner
♥ Powers of observation – a summary of the recovery from Love Addiction
♥ Every day is a good day, especially for you – looking after yourself in every way

As we have seen, Love Addiction tends to co-exist with codependence. It is a compulsive, drive towards love – or idealised love. Love Addiction is painful and disturbing, not only for the Love Addict but also for everyone associated with her. It wreaks not only emotional damage but also damage to physical health and financial chaos. Consider the effect upon your body of all the time spent obsessing about the love partner, in terms of worry, stress and anxiety. My own health has suffered greatly during my addiction. I have seen it many times in my practice, where a client has become so entrenched in their Love Addiction that she has compromised her health in order to cling to their love fantasy.

Beyond Love Addiction

Ask yourself now how much time has been spent on a relationship, neglecting things of greater importance, such as family duties, daily care of the children and your own health and career choices? Have your family and other relationships suffered? Most importantly, has the self, you, been neglected?

Divorce devastates families emotionally, socially and financially, limiting choices and affecting the security of a healthy lifestyle within a family unit. More and more people are living single lives, further isolating themselves. What message are we sending our children? How can we expect them to thrive if they follow our example? For this reason alone, it is crucial to recover and begin healthy relating. You will surely find a more joyful way of living your life and staying grounded in reality.

It is important that you acknowledge your need for support as a human being suffering from a devastating dis-ease. Continuing support from your therapist and support groups (see end of the book) will prove valuable and merits a committed heart and mind from you.

How can we learn new ways in which to love healthily? It is your new life challenge to do things differently. I want to love in a healthy, adult way and my wish for you is that you now have the skills from this book to do so, too. S-l-o-w the whole relationship process down. This may well be different to past experiences. Beware intensity: it is not intimacy. Intimacy, ('In To Me See', to quote Robert Burney) is a process that is gentle, respectful and non intrusive.

Intimacy without addiction

Intimacy implies sharing with another person the real you and listening to that person as you learn who they are.

- ♥ Sex is not intimacy. As you grow in your knowledge of each other, sex and lovemaking represent a natural progression in knowing and sharing more of each other
- ♥ Spend time exploring each other in loving non-sexual ways, maybe stroking each other's face and hair and stroking your partner's body, whispering affirmations to your partner as you do this.
- ♥ Encourage each other to talk about your feelings. Maybe you are feeling hurt or sad. Maybe you are feeling angry about something the other person did or said. Take the time to share your feelings in a gentle and honest way, in such a way that ensures trust and safety remain with you both.
- ♥ Consider carefully what you do and say.
- ♥ Use your powers of observation on yourself as well as on your partner. Share, for example, something that you noticed about your partner or yourself when an incident happened.
- ♥ Notice how loving your partner is towards you and acknowledge it. If your partner is putting you down or demeaning you in some way, share with your partner what you think about it and then how you feel about it. Perhaps, that you are feeling hurt and that you do not like it. State how you would prefer things to be between you.

Powers of observation

Observing yourself in almost everything that you do in important relationships helps you put in place limits and boundaries.

Begin a running documentary in your mind, observing what is happening as it happens. Think to yourself 'Isn't it interesting when so and so does such and such, his/her face changes or s/he becomes...' By doing this, you can begin to separate yourself from anxiety and keep yourself grounded, taking care to be respectful of your partner with any observations you wish to share.

♥ I advocate clear communication, not interpretation of another's actions. Ask for clarity from the other person; reflect it back if necessary to make sure communication and understanding are as accurate as possible.

♥ List your warning signs, what attracts you in a partner, know what hooks you in and put boundaries in place to keep you from the familiar patterns. Be bold enough to protect yourself from abusive situations, and be firm about your boundaries. Get used to saying 'No'. Practise if necessary and test yourself, too, in a private experiment. (See also Chapter 9: *Recognising boundaries in relationships*.)

♥ What age do you think your inner child is in this relationship? Remember that your inner child needs your parenting skills to nurture him/her – not someone else's caretaking skills. If your inner child is distressed by your partner, you may be regressing into an unhealthy state. Remind yourself that you are an adult and challenge any immature feelings. Accept your inner child, nurture her and simply acknowledge those feelings that belong to your past. (See Chapter 4: *Compassion in loss* and Chapter 5: *The burden of shame*.)

♥ Observe yourself in your new relationship: check that you are not putting in more energy than the relationship deserves at the beginning. How often are you calling? Are you the one making the arrangements? Question why you are doing this.

♥ If you are a codependent, you are likely to be attracted to addictive relationships. Addictive people choose codependent partners because they will be kept comfortable; the codependent partner will support the addict whatever the cost to himself or herself. (See Chapter 11: *Interdependence within love*.)

♥ Ask yourself if you are violating your beliefs by staying with this person. Continue to be vigilant with yourself. You may have been abandoned when you were a child, but it is imperative now that you stay grounded and continue to nurture both your inner child and the adult that you are now. (See Chapter 5: *The burden of shame*).

♥ Accept the fear of vulnerability and challenge yourself with your thoughts and behaviours of the past. Remind yourself that doing things differently may be uncomfortable at first and that is a sign that you are actively changing old behaviours and thought patterns. In time your new ways of thinking and behaving will become integrated in a healthy, positive, nurturing way

♥ Anger needs to be accepted and expressed appropriately to prevent a build up of anger and ultimately an explosion of rage. (See Chapter 3: *The balance of emotional energy* for how to release anger.)

♥ Take the time, when you are alone, to write a letter (do not send) to the person you think abandoned you when you were a child. Write about the saddest time for you when you were a child. Write as many times as you need to, to release any charged, repressed energy, as I explained in detail in Chapter 4: *Compassion in loss* in the section entitled 'Moving forward from grief to compassion'.

♥ Learn and believe that you – as well as others – deserve respect.

♥ Changing the negative by replacing it with the positive is a vital yet simple method of buliding self-esteem and reducing shame and anxiety. Select some positive affirmations from Chapter 8: *Affirming your self and your beliefs.* (See also Chapter 6: *Self-esteem – learning to value yourself.*)

♥ Remember to have compassion for yourself: it has been a difficult journey but you are now on the way to recovery. (See Chapter 4: *Compassion in loss.*)

♥ Above all, always keep in mind the authenticity of your relationship. (See Chapter 10: *Reality – living in truth.*)

Every day is a good day – specially for you

You can use your new self-empowerment skills to secure yourself a healthy loving relationship, firstly with yourself and then with others. As you begin to change your thoughts and behaviours, those close to you are likely to notice and perhaps reveal some of their own fears and emotional discomfort. The process is rather like throwing a stone into a pond, with the ripples reaching far beyond. It is important, however, that you don't deviate from your objective. Your journey may have its difficulties, but continue to affirm yourself and obtain support where you can.

Self-care is an essential element of your recovery and it is vital that you integrate it with your daily life. Here are some suggestions:

- ❤ Be aware of the type of partner you are typically drawn towards and actively challenge and withdraw from a compulsive attraction. Decline what you are now able to recognise as an impossible partner – for you.
- ❤ Reserve a special time for self-care so that you can enjoy the luxury – and deserved treat – that you have chosen to enhance your self.
- ❤ Follow a balanced eating plan with regular meals at about the same time each day. Do not binge or starve in response to your emotions.
- ❤ Take care to get enough sleep. Sleep may be disturbed during this time of self-discovery. Note down any dreams and thoughts upon waking. Sleep can be the best time for the subconscious mind to process information and painful issues.
- ❤ Understanding your physical responses to emotion can help you Identify your feelings.
- ❤ Take gentle exercise every day. If you prefer more strenuous exercise, or long country walks, limit yourself to no more than three or four times a week. The feel-good factor of regular exercise is undeniable, but there may be a risk of developing a new addiction, otherwise called a cross addiction – exercise in this case – in place of the old one.
- ❤ Try T'ai Chi, Pilates or yoga; they may help to enhance your balance and breathing techniques and can be very effective tools in achieving balance.
- ❤ Remember your daily affirmations, a vital part of exchanging the condemning inner voice of the past for a new, positive reality.

- Consider a detox plan at a spa or health club.
- Deep tissue massage may help with unresolved trauma. Be prepared for feeling sensitive after a detox massage. If you feel sad or angry, for example, acknowledge and accept these feelings. Perhaps begin to process their origins. Allow your body to experiencee the pain as it expels old hurts. Don't worry if you start to cry during a massage: an experienced therapist will understand this. Take this release of emotion as an encouraging sign of your mind and body working together.
- Give yourself special treats – such as massage, facial, manicure and visits to the hairdresser – as part of a regular programme that confirms you are precious and worthwhile.
- Rekindle your inner child and satisfy your creative side; take up the hobbies you used to enjoy in earlier days.
- Reserve time in your diary for trips away. Visit friends and relatives near and far.

To love is to be vulnerable in a healthy way, not because we haven't used appropriate boundaries or because we have lost ourselves in Love Addiction. However, if you are not currently in a relationship do not enter into a new one for a sound period of time, perhaps a year or until you feel you have rebuilt your self-esteem and learned enough to keep yourself protected and safe with the use of boundaries.

A healthy relationship takes time and if it's truly healthy it will last – there is no hurry. Love the experience of the beginning of your relationship. If you are recovering while in an existing relationship, there is nevertheless a new you emerging and therefore a new phase of the relationship. There is a big difference between loving an experience and loving another person. Keep yourself anchored and be true to your self: never abandon the essential you.

My intention has been to offer you, the reader, a journey through Love Addiction and I hope that you may have identified your self and some of the patterns you make in love relationships. By doing this, you will be able to address the self-defeating patterns that may have caused you stress and heartache in the past. I wish you well upon your journey of life and love.

KEY POINTS

- ♥ Do not abandon your self
- ♥ Take care of your self with compassion
- ♥ Intimacy, vulnerability and love need boundaries.

REFERENCES

Bradshaw, J (2005) *Healing the shame that binds you.* New York: Recovery Classic.

Carnes, Patrick J (1997) *The betrayal bond – breaking free of exploitative relationships.* Florida, USA: Health Communications Inc.

Pert, Candace B (1997) *Molecules of emotions – why you feel the way you feel.* London, UK: Simon & Schuster.

BIBLIOGRAPHY

The books listed below have all helped me on my personal journal and have provided some of the insight I needed into making sense of my struggles. Through these readings I have been able better to understand the cycle I was in and thereby write *The Love Trap*. In particular, I would recommend the writings of Patrick Carnes for further understanding of trauma and attachment and repetitive cycles; Candace Pert for how the body holds emotional pain; John Bradshaw for generational influence; and Pia Mellody for the cycles within dysfunctional love relationships.

Books

Bradshaw, John (1995) *Family Secrets: What You Don't Know Can Hurt You* New York: Random House

Bradshaw, John (2005) *Healing the Shame that Binds You* New York: Recovery Classics. (Originally published by Health Communications Inc, Florida, 1989)

Carnes, Patrick 1997 *The Betrayal Bond* Florida: Health Communications Inc

Mellody, Pia, Wells Miller, Andrea, Miller, J Keith (1989) *Facing Codependence: What It Is, Where It Comes From, How It Sabotages Our Lives.* New York: Barnes & Noble

Mellody Pia, Wells Miller, Andrea, Miller, J Keith 1992 *Facing Love Addiction: Giving Yourself the Power to Change the Way You Love* San Francisco: Harper (an imprint of HarperCollins, New York)

Pert, Candace B 1997 *Molecules of Emotion – The Science of Mind-Body Medicine* New York: Simon & Schuster

Worden, J William 2004 *Grief Counselling and Grief Therapy: A Handbook for the Mental Health Practitioner* 3rd edition. London: Routledge

Journals

The New Scientist
Weekly science and technology news magazine available from newsagents and: www.newscientist.com

UK/Rest of world
Tel. +44 (0)1444 475636 (9 am to 5 pm BST)
Email: ns.subs@qss-uk.com
USA/Canada
Tel. 888 822 3242 (9 am to 5 pm EST)
Email: subscribe@newscientist.com

Australia/New Zealand
Tel. + 02 9422 2666 / 1300 360126
Email: subscriptions@newscientist.com.au

The British Association for Counselling and Psychotherapy
publishes two journals: *Therapy Today* magazine and *Counselling and Psychotherapy Research*

BACP House
Unit 15 St John's Business Park, Lutterworth
Leicestershire LE17 4HB
Phone 0870 443 5252
Fax 0870 443 5161
Email: bacp@bacp.co.uk

See also *Support Groups*, with their websites and publications.

SUPPORT GROUPS

Support groups around the world can offer you additional help, enabling you to live your life with healthy self-esteem and relationships that are manageable and joyful to you and to your extended family and friends. The great benefit of these support groups is that you can reach them by email or by visiting their websites, no matter in which country you live or how isolated your home.

Global

www.allaboutlove.org/loveaddiction

www.codependents.org (The CoDA World Fellowship)

www.healthymind.com

www.love-addiction.com

www.loveaddicts.org

www.loveandaddiction.com

www.samaritans.org (for confidential emotional support)

UK

For all types of addiction

Priory Healthcare
Priory Central Office
Priory House
Randalls Way
Leatherhead
Surrey
KT22 7TP
Tel: 01372 860 400
Email: info@priorygroup.com
www.prioryhealthcare.uk

For bullying, shame and PTSD

Bullying results in fear, shame, embarrassment and guilt, which increase while the bullying continues. Bullies recognise these symptoms and use them to disempower their victim.

www.bullyonline.org

For confidential emotional support

Samaritans
Tel: 08457 90 90 90
www.samaritans.org.uk

For counselling about relationship problems

RELATE
Tel: 0845 456 1310 or +44 (0) 1788 573241
www.relate.org.uk

Sex and Love Addicts Anonymous United Kingdom
For details of meetings:
www.slaaonline.org and www.slaauk.com

and for meetings in Northern Ireland:
www.slaa-ireland.ie

USA

For confidential emotional support

Samaritans
www.samaritans.com

COSLAA
This is a 12-step support group for the recovery of family, friends, and significant others whose lives have been affected by their relationship with someone addicted to sex and/or love. COSLAA, also known as CO-Sex and Love Addicts Anonymous, reaches out to the suffering individual who is 18 years or older, regardless of sexual orientation, gender, or relationship status.

COSLAA Help Line for newcomers is:
860-456-0032
www.coslaa.org

S-Anon
S-Anon is a 12-step recovery program for those who have been affected by someone else's sexual behaviour. S-Anon is based on the Twelve Steps and the Twelve Traditions of Alcoholics Anonymous:

P.O. Box 111242
Nashville, TN 37222-1242
Tel: (800) 210-8141 or (615) 833-3152
Email: sanon@sanon.org
www.sanon.org

www.sexualrecovery.com

SLAA
Sex and Love Addicts Anonymous, 12-step recovery program
www.slaafws.org

Emotional trauma

The Meadows
Extended-care facility to provide ongoing care with a focus on trauma resolution:

The Meadows, Arizona
Tels: Toll-free: 800-MEADOWS (800-632-3697)
        Outside the US: 928-684-3926
www.themeadows.org

INDEX